Safety and the year 2000

J Henderson and G I Davidson
Real Time Engineering Ltd
Academy House
Academy Park
Gower Street
Glasgow G51 1PR

The 'year 2000 problem' is fairly well-known and relatively simple to describe. Many computers and software applications recognise dates (eg 1999) by two digits only (eg 99). At the change of date to the year 2000, some will recognise the date as 1990, or as another default date. Systems may then produce incorrect results or fail completely. The failure of one system will affect the others to which it is connected.

This change from 1999 to 2000 is the most readily recognised problem but there is a more general problem associated with what is called 'date discontinuity'. Date discontinuity occurs when the time (as expressed by a system or its software) does not successfully move forward in line with true time. It is the nature of date discontinuity that it may cause simultaneous failures of processes. This may put additional demands on safety systems which may not have been designed to handle multiple, apparently unrelated, failures.

This document addresses the problem presented to users of real time, safety-related control systems which may be vulnerable to date discontinuity in general and failure at the year 2000 in particular. It provides guidance on one method of approach which users can adopt to identify vulnerable systems and then rectify problems in order to meet their legal health and safety obligations. Although aimed primarily at safety-related systems, the methods used to assess vulnerability can be adapted to address the potential for failure of other related systems.

This report and the work it describes were funded by the Health and Safety Executive (HSE). Its contents, including any opinions and/or conclusions expressed, are those of the authors alone and do not necessarily reflect HSE policy.

Real Time Engineering Ltd, its officers, employees and agents (on behalf of whom this notice is issued) shall be under no liability or responsibility in negligence or otherwise howsoever to any person in respect of any inaccuracy herein or omission herefrom, or in respect of any act or omission which is caused or contributed to this report being issued with the information or advice it contains.

Without derogating from the generality of the foregoing, neither Real Time Engineering Ltd nor its officers, employees or agents shall be liable in negligence or otherwise howsoever for any indirect or consequential loss to any person caused by or arising from any information, advice, inaccuracy, or omission being given or contained herein for any act or omission causing or contributing to any such information, advice, inaccuracy, or omission being given or contained herein.

HSE BOOKS

© *Crown copyright 1998*
Applications for reproduction should be made in writing to:
Copyright Unit, Her Majesty's Stationery Office,
St Clements House, 2-16 Colegate, Norwich NR3 1BQ

First published 1998

ISBN 0 7176 1491 3

All rights reserved. No part of this publication may be reproduced, stored in a retrieval system, or transmitted in any form or by any means (electronic, mechanical, photocopying, recording or otherwise) without the prior written permission of the copyright owner.

SAFETY AND THE YEAR 2000

Preface by HSE

1. This report is intended to help users of software-based equipment understand the problem associated with the year 2000 and to provide them with a strategy for tackling it. The problem has been variously referred to in the press as 'The Millennium Bug', 'The Millennium Time-bomb', or the Year 2000 (Y2K) Problem.

2. Although the problem *is* real, its extent and possible effects for safety-related control systems can only be established through thorough investigation. A reasoned approach is essential to solving the problem. To do nothing in the hope that there will not be an increased risk to health and safety is not an option. ***The message from this report is to begin your investigation without delay.***

Introducing the problem

3. The 'Year 2000 Problem' is fairly well-known and relatively simple to state. Many computers and other software applications represent the year number (eg 1999) by two digits only (eg 1999 would be represented as 99). At the change to the year 2000, a two-digit year number will change from 99 to 00, which some software may recognise as the year 1900. More generally, an incorrect year change or recognition will produce unpredictable results. Date-dependent systems may then produce incorrect results or fail completely if these incorrect year numbers are used in arithmetical calculations.

4. This change from 1999 to 2000 is the most readily-recognised problem but you should be aware that there is a more general problem associated with what is called 'date discontinuity'. Date discontinuity occurs when the time (as expressed by a system or its software), does not successfully move forward in line with true time.

5. For instance, some software systems are equipped with 'clocks' which calculate time from a fixed point (eg by counting the number of clock ticks since 1 January 1980 or some other arbitrary date of significance to the manufacturer). When the register which accumulates these clock ticks is full, it will overflow (like a car odometer) and show zero. This will be interpreted by the software as the fixed date of origin ie 1980.

6. There is also a special case associated with the fact that the year 2000 is a leap year. ***(Please pay no attention to anyone who tells you otherwise).*** Some systems are incorrectly programmed for this and risk failure at 29 February, 2000 or 31 December 2000 (the 366th day). This particular type of error in programming has already resulted in the failure of a computer-based process control system. It occurred at the end of 1996 at an aluminium smelting plant in New Zealand. Although the safety of personnel was not affected in this incident, it serves to demonstrate that control systems

are susceptible to date discontinuity.

7. Date discontinuity as a topic, and specific dates which are likely to cause problems are described in the report. ***It is important that guidance on how to cope with the 'Year 2000 Problem' should be applied with equal vigour to other date discontinuity problems.***

Types of systems affected

8. The problem potentially exists in every type of Programmable Electronic System (PES) - personal computers, mainframe and mini computers, programmable logic controllers, microprocessors and 'embedded' software-based systems. Embedded systems can be difficult to recognise but generally comprise some type of microprocessor or digital electronics, often with a timer, and are 'ernbedded' (built-into) many modern instruments, controllers and machinery. The program held within embedded systems is not normally accessible for modification by the user.

The sources of the problem

9. The 'Year 2000 Problem' can have its sources in any of the layers which make up software- based systems. These are the clock mechanism, the operating system, the software packages, libraries and tools and the application software. Each of these layers and their possible vulnerability to date discontinuity are described in the report.

The effect on safety

10. In most engineering, production and manufacturing environments, a variety of systems are used to plan, measure, store information, control processes and to keep them safe. These systems are often referred to as 'real time' systems because data (events) are processed as they occur, the results being available immediately. Quite often such systems are linked together by communications networks which means that information is shared and used for different purposes.

11. When such information is both time or date-dependent *and* important for the safe operation of a process or machine, then safety becomes an issue at year 2000. Also, the correct operation of a safety system which is itself resilient to the 'Year 2000 Problem' may still be affected by the failure of a subsidiary system to which it is linked.

12. The unpalatable fact is that the 'Year 2000 Problem' is a failure which is potentially common to all systems. In the jargon of the control systems world, this is known as a 'common cause' failure, ie it can cause the simultaneous failure of more that one system. In the case of year 2000, the potential exists for a very great many systems to fail at the same time.

13. In summary, the nature of the 'Year 2000 Problem' means that any programmable electronic system within a linked chain of processes may fail and so could affect any safety-related

arrangements. Equipment containing embedded systems may fail or give incorrect information. The results of calculations may be erroneous and operators may take inappropriate action, or other dependent safety-related control circuits may respond inappropriately. Note also that the methodology in this report is applicable to any computer - based system whether operating in a 'real time' environment or not.

What you can do now

14. Complete the steps in the decision tree adjacent; the result will indicate the options open to you.

Safety at work and the law

15. Suppliers, employers, the self- employed and consultants have legal obligations. These are set out in general terms in the Health and Safety at Work etc. Act 1974 (HSWA) and the Supply of Machinery (Safety) Regulations 1992 as amended. Other aspects relating to consumer safety are covered by the Consumer Protection Act 1987 (CPA) but HSE's concern is safety in the workplace and this report concentrates on that.

Duty of employers

16. Section 2 (1) of HSWA in particular places a duty on employers to ensure, so far as is reasonably practicable, the health, safety and welfare of their employees.

17. Section 3 of HSWA requires employers and the self-employed to ensure, so far as is reasonably practicable, the health and safety of others who may be affected by their work activities. This also covers the work of consultants who provide advice and technical support to their customers.

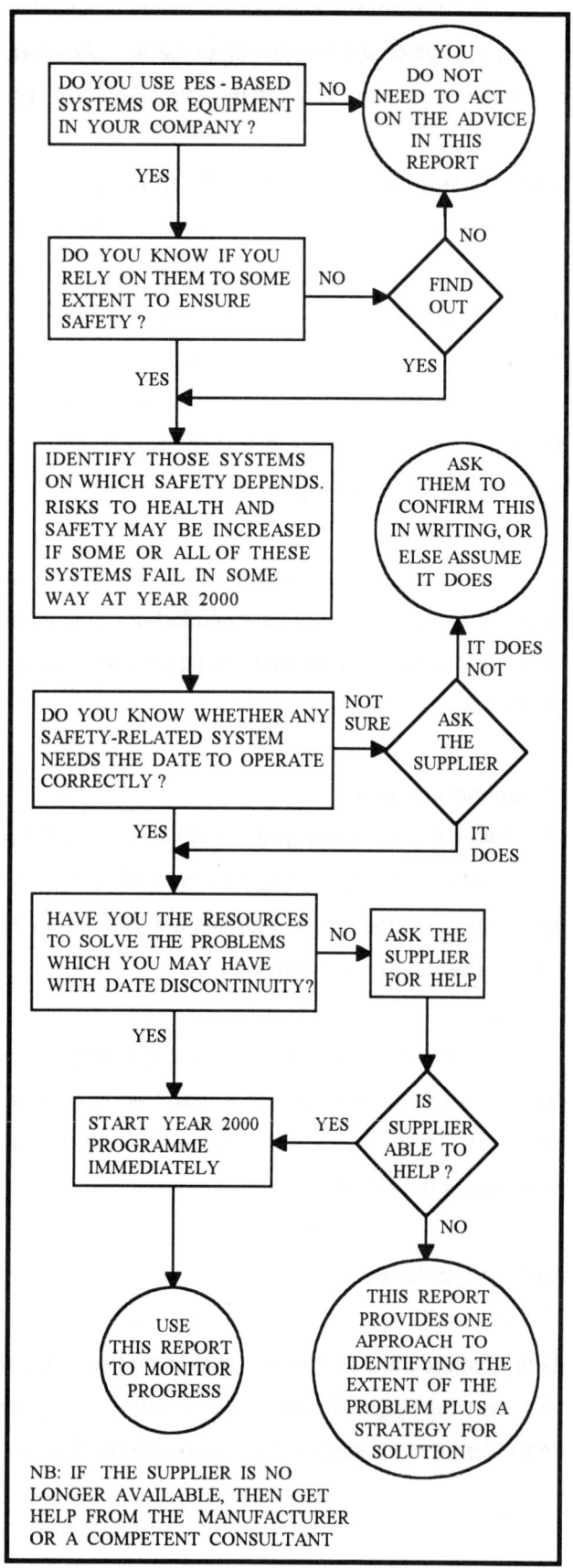

v

18. Other, more specific legislation, relating to control systems is the Provision and Use of Work Equipment Regulations 1992 (PUWER). Regulation 5 requires that work equipment must be suitable by design, construction or adaptation, for its intended purpose. Regulation 18 requires that employers ensure, so far as is reasonably practicable, that the operation of a control system does not pose any additional risk to health or safety. Any hazardous event which may result from a date discontinuity problem in a safety - related control system may therefore contravene this regulation.

Duty of designers, manufacturers and suppliers

19. Those who design, manufacture or supply articles for use at work also have a duty to those who use those articles (section 6 of HSWA). This duty extends to the information provided for use. It also extends to the revision of such information if it becomes known that anything gives rise to a risk to health or safety. In other words the law requires designers, manufacturers and suppliers to be pro-active and take reasonably practicable steps to inform their customers of potential problems once they become known. Date-discontinuity problems in the hardware or software of a safety-related control system is such a problem.

20. Manufacturers and suppliers also have more specific duties under the Supply of Machinery (Safety) Regulations 1992 as amended, for machines that have control systems. In particular a fault in the control circuit logic such as a date discontinuity problem, should not lead to dangerous conditions.

Recommendations

21. If you use or provide your employees with PES on which you rely for safety, then the following report will provide you with one method for tackling the 'Year 2000 Problem'. Do not assume that your safety-related control systems are immune to date discontinuity problems: remember it is much better to be safe than sorry.

22. Do not wait for someone to develop a simple 'magic method' which will solve this problem. The consensus of technical opinion is that it would have surfaced by now if it were at all possible.
Act now: as far as safety is concerned this is ***not*** tomorrow's problem - time, in this case, is most definitely of the essence !

Further guidance

23. HSE will issue a free guidance leaflet on this topic in the Spring of 1998.
This guidance and further information on this topic, will be available from the Internet (address: http://www.open.gov.uk/hse/hsehome.htm). The guidance will be based on the material in this report and will give more specific advice on what HSE expects of dutyholders.

CONTENTS

1. EXECUTIVE SUMMARY 1

2. INTRODUCTION 3
   2.1 PURPOSE OF THIS DOCUMENT 3
   2.2 TERMS OF REFERENCE 4
   2.3 CONDUCT OF THE STUDY 4
   2.4 DEFINITIONS 4

3. NATURE OF PROBLEM 7
   3.1 INTRODUCTION 7
   3.2 THE DATE PROBLEM 7
   3.3 WHAT ARE THE SOURCES OF THE PROBLEM? 7
   3.4 HOW CAN THIS PROBLEM AFFECT SAFETY? 8
   3.5 WHICH SYSTEMS ARE VULNERABLE? 10
   3.6 ASSESSING CRITICALITY OF PES IN TERMS OF IMPACT ON SAFETY 13
   3.7 ASSESSING THE FUNCTIONALITY OF PES 14
   3.8 ASSESSING THE CONSTRUCTION OF PES 15
   3.9 OVERALL VULNERABILITY ASSESSMENT - DECISION SEQUENCE AND CHECKLISTS 15
   3.10 OVERALL SYSTEM VULNERABILITY MAPPING 32
   3.11 APPLYING THE RESULTS OF THE VULNERABILITY MAPPING 33

4. APPROACH TO SOLVING THE PROBLEM 35
   4.1 INTRODUCTION 35
   4.2 THE PROGRAMME 35
   4.3 PROGRAMME MANAGEMENT 36
   4.4 ROLES AND RESPONSIBILITIES 37

5. AUDIT AND ANALYSIS STAGE 41
   5.1 INTRODUCTION 41
   5.2 AUDIT OUTLINE 41
   5.3 PREPARATION 41
   5.4 INVENTORY 42
   5.5 IMPACT ASSESSMENT 44
   5.6 INITIAL REVIEW 44
   5.7 SUPPLIER CONTACT 45
   5.8 FOLLOW-UP REVIEW 47
   5.9 TESTING DECISIONS 47
   5.10 INVESTIGATIVE TESTING 47
   5.11 ANALYSIS 49

6. STRATEGY AND PLANNING STAGE 51
   6.1 INTRODUCTION 51
   6.2 DECISION MAKING 51
   6.3 STRATEGIES 51
   6.4 PROJECT PLANS 53
   6.5 ACCEPTANCE CRITERIA 54
   6.6 METHODS AND WORKING PRACTICES 54
   6.7 CONTINGENCY PLANNING 54

7.	IMPLEMENTATION AND TEST STAGE		55
	7.1	INTRODUCTION	55
	7.2	IMPLEMENTATION PROGRAMME MANAGEMENT	55
	7.3	IMPLEMENTATION	55
	7.4	ACCEPTANCE CRITERIA	57
	7.5	TESTING	58
	7.6	YEAR 2000 READINESS	60
8.	RESOURCING THE YEAR 2000 PROGRAMME		63
	8.1	INTRODUCTION	63
	8.2	MANPOWER RESOURCES	63
	8.3	TEST EQUIPMENT AND TEST ENVIRONMENT	63
	8.4	EXTERNAL TECHNICAL ASSISTANCE	63
APPENDIX A			65
APPENDIX B			67
APPENDIX C			69
APPENDIX D			75

1. EXECUTIVE SUMMARY

The "Year 2000 Problem" is fairly well-known, and relatively simple. Many computers and software applications recognise dates (e.g., 1999) by two digits only (e.g., 99). At the change of date to the Year 2000, some will recognise the date as 1900, or as another default date. Systems may then produce incorrect results or fail completely. The failure of one system may affect the others to which it is connected.

The consequences of the problem have been recognised for financial and business systems, and for desktop PCs. It is, however, less widely understood that the Year 2000 problem equally affects real-time and embedded systems, such as local controllers, monitoring systems, distributed control systems, production management systems, machinery and equipment containing these systems and so on. Many engineering and manufacturing companies depend on such systems, and whole processes may be at risk. The problem affects large and small enterprises without discrimination.

In production environments, safety often depends upon, or is strongly influenced by, the successful operation of control systems. If these systems are vulnerable because of date-handling problems, safety could be compromised.

In addition, the nature of the Year 2000 problem is such that it may cause simultaneous failures of processes. This will inevitably put additional demand on safety systems which, in some cases, are not designed to handle multiple, apparently unrelated, failures.

Finally, the safety of a process may ultimately depend on the continuing supply of a service (externally or internally produced) such as cooling water, power, lubricant, inert gas, removal of waste or waste heat, etc. In these cases, safety can be compromised if a Year 2000 problem causes the failure of the service.

Even for simple systems, the authors have identified Year 2000 failures in a significant minority of cases. As functionality increases, so does the potential for Year 2000 failure, and the authors advise that the failure rate rises considerably above 50% for more sophisticated systems (note that these may or may not be safety systems). The potential failure of real-time, safety-related control systems as a result of Year 2000 problems should be taken very seriously, and organisations should deal directly and swiftly with the topic.

This document addresses how best to identify vulnerable real-time, safety-related control systems, and provides guidance on a strategy which users can adopt to rectify problems, and hence meet their legal health and safety obligations. Although aimed primarily at safety-related systems, the methods used to assess vulnerability can be adapted to address the potential for failure of other related systems.

2. INTRODUCTION

2.1 PURPOSE OF THIS DOCUMENT

The aim of this document is to provide guidance and pragmatic advice to individuals and teams addressing the Year 2000 problem as it affects real-time, safety-related control systems.

Although it may seem that the major impact of the Year 2000 problems will be on large companies with complex interacting systems, many small and medium-sized enterprises (SMEs) make use of real-time and embedded systems to control and monitor their manufacturing or production processes, and some of these systems contribute to safety. The guidelines are intended to apply to large and small organisations alike. The terms used are intended to be generic and may differ from those used in specific industry sectors.

The guidelines are unavoidably detailed in some technical areas, such is the nature of the problem. Some organisations will carry all of the technical skills required to apply the guidelines. However, it is probable that some SMEs will not have the appropriate internal expertise available, in which case the guidelines can be used as a source of the technical and safety topics which will enable an SME to manage the problem successfully by ensuring that the topics are addressed by equipment suppliers, maintainers and external systems consultants in their rectification of the Year 2000 problem for real-time, safety-related systems.

2.1.1 Who should read this document?

Successful rectification of the Year 2000 problem requires the application of a variety of skills:-

- it requires an understanding of the structure of programmable electronic systems (PES) - IT systems, PLCs and embedded systems, and the technical skills to rectify the problem;

- it requires an appreciation of the impact which systems have on safety within the workplace, and of how systems can be upgraded without compromising safety during or after the rectification process;

- it requires a detailed knowledge of the production or engineering environment, and of how the Year 2000 rectification programme can be accommodated within the production schedule;

- it requires knowledge of the economics of the production process, in order that essential rectification work can be carried out while minimising the impact on the organisational finances.

So handling the Year 2000 problem for real-time, safety-related control systems needs this essential combination of safety, IT, production/engineering, and business skills. In small companies, some of these skills, or at least the responsibility for the area of business requiring these skills, may well be combined in the role of a single individual. In larger organisations, each role may be discharged by a different individual or team.

This document addresses safety, IT and production topics, and provides guidance in each area. We suggest therefore that the document should be read by all of those who have responsibilities and authority to act in these areas, i.e., safety managers, IT managers, production managers and business decision-makers.

In the first instance, this document should be read by Technical Directors **and** the person responsible for computer systems.

2.2 TERMS OF REFERENCE

The Health and Safety Executive (HSE) recognises that real-time processes, manufacturing systems and information-based systems controlled by computers may be subject to unreliable performance as a result of the Year 2000 problem, and similar date discontinuity problems. HSE considers it important to assess whether the use of such systems in safety-related applications poses any additional risk to health and safety.

HSE has commissioned this report in order to provide users with one method of approach regarding:-

- an appropriate strategy to employ to identify the problem;
- an appropriate strategy to employ in tackling the problem;
- what needs to be done to meet their legal obligations.

2.3 CONDUCT OF THE STUDY

The information presented in this report has been gathered over the period from July to October 1997, and is based upon interviews with experts in a variety of industrial sectors, published material, and the authors' experience arising from their contribution to a number of Year 2000 rectification programmes in engineering and manufacturing environments.

The authors wish to acknowledge the valuable contribution made by the following organisations who freely gave their time to assist the authors in the development of this report:-

- British Airways;
- Institution of Electrical Engineers;
- Magnox Electric;
- National Air Traffic Services;
- Railtrack;
- Scottish Nuclear;
- Shell UK Exploration and Production.

The parties with whom the authors have had discussions have not been given the opportunity to review the report nor to state whether they agree or disagree with any of its content.

A number of case studies are summarised in Appendix C. Although individual companies and suppliers are not named, for reasons of confidentiality, the systems failures identified are based on real situations.

2.4 DEFINITIONS

This document refers to "programmable electronic systems" and "programmable electronics", which can be defined as follows:-

- A **programmable electronic system (PES)** is a system for control, protection or monitoring based on one or more programmable electronic (PE) devices, including all elements of the system such as power suppliers, sensors and other input devices, data highways and other communication paths, and actuators and other output devices.

- A **programmable electronic (PE)** is based on computer technology which may comprise of hardware, software, and of input and/or output units. This term covers microelectronic devices based on one or more central processing units (CPUs) together with associated memories, etc. Examples of a PE are microprocessors, microcontrollers, smart sensors, transmitters and actuators.

3. NATURE OF PROBLEM

3.1 INTRODUCTION

This section introduces the date problem, and identifies its root causes. We explore how the existence of the Year 2000 problem is likely to impact on safety in a variety of environments, and outline a method of assessing the vulnerability of systems, and the potential effect which their failure will have on safety.

3.2 THE DATE PROBLEM

The root of the problem lies in the common usage of only two digits to identify the year portion of a date, e.g., 21/10/97, instead of 21/10/1997. This is a widespread style, and has been used for many years by manufacturers, programmers and users of computer systems.

As a result, many operating systems, packages and applications now use two-digit year fields to determine time, and to perform time-based calculations. At the Year 2000, systems and software based on this approach will identify the year as "00", with the result that an event occurring in 1999 will be calculated as having happened -99 years ago ("00" - "99"). Calculations will go awry, systems may fail, and whole processes may be affected.

This is the most readily-recognised "Year 2000" problem, but readers should be aware that there is a more general problem associated with what is called "date discontinuity". Date discontinuity occurs when the time as expressed by a system or its software does not successfully move forward in line with true time.

For instance, the clocks of some systems calculate time as an offset from a fixed point (i.e., number of clock ticks since a fixed time and date). When the register which counts up these clock ticks overflows, the register will revert to 0, and the system clock will revert to its fixed origin date. There are a variety of systems based on this principle.

There is also a special case associated with the fact that the Year 2000 is a leap year (and please pay no attention to anyone who tells you otherwise!). Some systems and applications are incorrectly programmed in this regard, and risk failure at 29 February 2000 or 31 December 2000 (the 366th day). Indeed, one of the best-known date discontinuity problems occurred on 31 December 1996, when systems at an aluminium smelter plant in New Zealand were unable to handle the leap year's 366th day, with considerable consequences (see Appendix C).

Date discontinuity as a whole, and specific dates which are likely to cause problems, are described in detail in Appendix A. In reading this document, please assume that the guidance which we provide for the "Year 2000" problem should be applied with equal vigour to handling other date discontinuity problems.

3.3 WHAT ARE THE SOURCES OF THE PROBLEM?

The Year 2000 problem can have its source in any of the layers which make up real-time or embedded systems, i.e.:-

- **clock mechanism;**

- **operating system;**

- **programming support tools;**

- **application software.**

All real-time systems, and virtually all embedded systems, incorporate some form of **clock mechanism**. The clock is normally mains or crystal controlled, and is often battery-backed. The clock can be initialised at the factory, or can be initialised each time the system is started up, or can be set at periodic intervals by an external source (e.g., Rugby MSF clock, another system or from a satellite or national time signal). The clock will often have a calendar function associated with it. Many store the year as only two digits. In addition, in very simple embedded systems, the calendar function may be erroneous (e.g., fails to handle leap Year 2000), and problems may result.

In simpler systems (such as microcontrollers or smart sensors), the time is often maintained by a hardware 'real-time clock' which stores and updates the time and date via a set of registers accessible to the processor. These systems use timers instead of real time clocks for most purposes.

More complex systems maintain time and date via an interface between the hardware and an **operating system** (the most primitive but not necessarily least complex layer of software in the system). Such systems generally contain basic firmware which also has access to the real-time clock. In a PC this is the BIOS, and in microcomputers it is often referred to as a virtual console interface.

Operating systems may also support 'software' based clock facilities which carry out calendar maintenance.

Any or all of these mechanisms are contained in real-time systems, and some do not successfully handle the Year 2000 problem. In some systems, the hardware and software elements can fail in different ways and/or then interact inappropriately.

The next layer of potential failure within a real-time or embedded system comprises the **programming support tools** (e.g., packages, libraries and tools) which are used by the software application. Some packages and libraries contain standard routines which read the date and time from the operating system, and many return the year in a 2-digit format. Some provide functions which are time-based (e.g., standard trend analysis in a SCADA package, or alarm/event time stamping in a PLC) and these are prone to failure at Year 2000.

The highest layer of potential failure is the **application software** level. In every system, the software written at this level is highly bespoke, i.e., it has been developed for one specific purpose. The methods by which dates are handled will vary from system to system as they have been developed at different times by different teams. Indeed, within a single system, it is quite feasible that a variety of mechanisms are used to retrieve, set and manipulate dates, some of which will be Year 2000-resilient, and some of which will not be.

3.4 HOW CAN THIS PROBLEM AFFECT SAFETY?

The main reason why safety can be compromised by the Year 2000 problem is that the problem potentially exists in every type of Programmable Electronic System (PES), and not just in PCs or mainframe computers. So Year 2000 failures can be present in minicomputers and microprocessors, in Programmable Logic Controllers (PLCs), and in many types of embedded system. Embedded systems can be difficult to recognise, but generally comprise some type of microprocessor or special-to-purpose digital circuitry, often with a timer, and are embedded within many modern instruments, controllers and machinery.

In most engineering, production and manufacturing environments, a variety of PES are used to plan, measure and control processes, and to keep them safe. **Simple instruments** (containing embedded systems) contribute to safety by measuring temperatures, pressures, speeds, rotation, vibration, and so on. Some more sophisticated **embedded systems** contribute to safety by building vibration profiles, measuring cracks and erosion, or undertaking trend analyses on rates of change of temperatures and pressures.

Local controllers and **PLCs** contribute to safety by measuring and checking plant conditions before taking actions which could have safety implications (e.g., opening/closing valves, stopping/starting machinery). **Minicomputers** contribute to safety by gathering data from local instruments, controllers and PLCs, and making that information available to operators, giving them a "big picture" of plant conditions, and providing facilities via which they can safely take control actions.

Safety protection systems (e.g., fire control systems, emergency shutdown systems) contribute to safety by taking executive action to make plant safe when it is considered to be in a dangerous condition. Safety protection systems also inform plant personnel of hazards, allowing evacuation of hazardous areas.

So a wide variety of PES can make a contribution to safety. If any of them are susceptible to the Year 2000 problem, then safety is undoubtedly compromised. The safety of an operation or process is usually assessed on the premise that common mode failure could result in one or at most two simultaneous failures. More widespread failure is generally guarded against by the use of redundancy, or diversity. In a redundant arrangement, a number of parallel PEs of identical functionality are constructed, such that if one fails, then a backup system immediately comes into play. In a diverse arrangement, PES constructed differently (but performing the same function) "vote" on action to be taken. However, since any PES may fail at the Year 2000, this style of protection is not sufficient in itself. Similarly, modular redundant voting systems based on the same technology are also at risk. Where a diverse technology is used, e.g., a mechanical, pneumatic, hydraulic system or electrical system (not including electronic systems) which performs the same function, this will not be affected by the Year 2000 problem.

Of course, it should also be remembered that safety can be compromised by failure of a PES not directly related to the process under review. Such PES include those which control or monitor:

- Cooling Water;

- Inert Gas;

- Waste or effluent disposal;

- Waste heat disposal;

- Video surveillance;

- Communications (telephone, radio, intercom);

- Fire/smoke detection;

- Energy supply (electricity, gas);

- Lubrication systems;

- Refrigerator/heating services;

- Air treatment plants;

- Emergency power (battery, generator, bottled gas).

In summary, the non-discriminatory nature of the Year 2000 problem means that any PES across the process chain may fail, with the result that safety arrangements may become inadequate. For instance, the temperatures, pressures, speeds, etc., measured by local instruments may not be correct, or the instruments may fail. The erosion details, or vibration profiles can no longer be trusted. The local controllers or PLCs may fail, or may initiate unsafe plant actions based on erroneous data received from instruments. Operators may be misled by incorrect information and take inappropriate actions, or may lose the "big picture" of plant status, which again can compromise safety. Finally, the safety protection PES themselves may become inoperable, if they use redundant or diverse electronic techniques.

The problems outlined above can result from a PES failure, or from the interconnectivity between or within PES (e.g., safety may be compromised by one PES feeding erroneous data to another). However, safety can also be affected by the interconnectivity of different elements within a process. Failure of an embedded or real-time system and its effect on other such systems is, of course, important, but we should not overlook the fact that the majority of processes, whether for production of a manufactured item or an energy product, are serially connected not by their systems, but by the process functionality itself.

Recent investigations have uncovered potential failures in areas where the knock-on effect of a minor PES has a major impact on safety and production, e.g.,

- A maritime radio distress system was found to be unable to handle the 29th February 2000. The result would have been that accurate positional data could not be transmitted in an emergency;

- An engine monitoring system was found to fail such that the most recent records (i.e., those taken in the Year 2000) were regarded as the oldest, and were discarded. The effect would be that dangerous wear and tear would go undetected, without warnings or alarms being raised;

- An H_2S analyser fails to operate correctly in the Year 2000. The effect would be failure to detect H_2S, a potentially lethal circumstance.

It should be noted that the above examples were unearthed as part of detailed Year 2000 investigations and generally can be (or in some cases already have been) remedied by fairly minor modifications to software and hardware. **Additional risks to health and safety will be possible only if the potential failures are not detected and addressed in an appropriate and timely manner.**

Year 2000 failure is probably the ultimate common mode fault, and can strike randomly across an entire process chain. Any previous assessment of process safety is negated by the Year 2000 problem. Waiting to see if it happens, and then fixing it if it does, is an unlikely option, because even if only a small percentage of the systems fail, the entire process could be halted or driven into an unsafe mode for a considerable period of time.

In short, it is very unlikely that a Year 2000 style problem was considered when the safety of most plant systems was last assessed. Consequently, a full review of safety in the light of the Year 2000 problem is strongly recommended.

3.5 WHICH SYSTEMS ARE VULNERABLE?

When assessing the impact on safety of Year 2000 failure of process systems within a production or engineering environment, it is essential that every PES (from the simplest instrument to the most sophisticated control and management system) is considered in full. However, some PES will have little or no impact on safety, and it will be possible to remove them from the assessment quickly (although if they impact on business integrity, you may wish to give them some priority nonetheless). Some PES will have no date dependencies, or will be able to operate entirely successfully because of their method of construction, and again these will have no adverse impact on safety.

To illustrate the systems which should be considered during a Year 2000 investigation, Figure 1 portrays a 'typical' factory with an illustration of a single process line and all related systems. It may be reasonable to say that some or even many of these will have no impact on safety if they fail, but such an assertion should be the result of active assessment and subsequent elimination of the system from consideration, not the result of instant judgement or accidental oversight.

In re-assessing safety, we need a mechanism by which to assess the vulnerability of systems and processes to Year 2000 failure. If we can identify at an early stage those PES which are most vulnerable, then we can prioritise actions successfully.

The **vulnerability of a system** can be determined by assessing the following factors:-

- its **criticality**: this is a measure of the importance of the system's contribution to safety and the effects of a system failure;

- its **functionality**: this is a measure of the dependence of the system on the successful manipulation of time-based information;

- its **construction**: this is a measure of the components of the system (hardware, software packages, tools) and their resilience to Year 2000 failure.

Obviously, if a PES makes a vital contribution to safety, is highly-dependent on dates, and is based on components known to cause Year 2000 failures, then it will be a very high priority in any rectification programme. At the other extreme, PES which score very low in this type of assessment can quickly be regarded as lesser priority items in the programme unless they can contribute to multiple system failures. (The failure of a single sensor may have no impact on safety. However, the failure of 30 sensors simultaneously could have a serious impact on safety.)

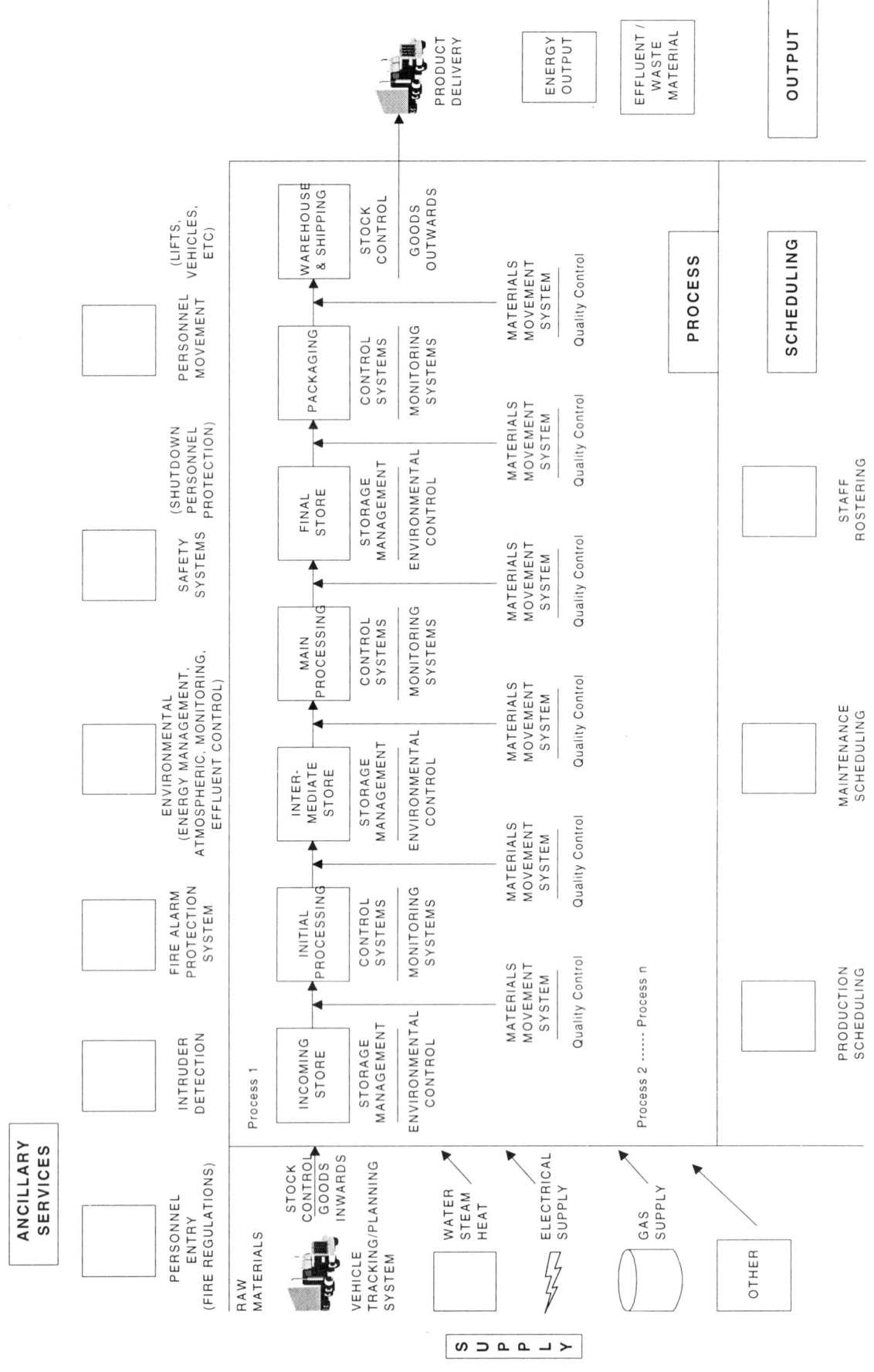

**Figure 1
Typical Factory**

3.6 ASSESSING CRITICALITY OF PES IN TERMS OF IMPACT ON SAFETY

When assessing the safety criticality of a PES, we need to identify the effect which it has on safety when operating within the total control scheme of the plant or machine. This relationship between control systems is often referred to as the control scheme "architecture".

To assess the possible effect of a PES failure on safety, we need to analyse, for each PES:-

- impact of its failure on other parts of the control system;

- impact of its failure on other systems, (PES and non-PES) which may be provided for plant or machine protection;

- impact of its failure on other PES with which it communicates or shares data.

Impact of Failure

"Failure" in this context includes the PES ceasing to work, producing incorrect (erroneous) outputs/results, or not responding correctly to input data, etc. The impact of a control system failure on plant, process or machinery is the same irrespective of what caused it to fail.

However, failure due to Year 2000 problems is a special case because it has the potential to effect many software-based systems simultaneously. In what follows, the impact of PES failure will be described in terms of Year 2000 problems, because that is the subject of this report.

In many cases, a PES affected by Year 2000 problems will continue to operate, but will perform erroneously. For instance, if the date or time is incorrect, or is being incorrectly processed within the system, then time-based calculations or analyses (e.g., averages, trends, maintenance scheduling) will be incorrectly performed. If a PES takes action as a result of such calculations, then those actions may be incorrect, and may jeopardise safety.

Impact on the Plant/Machine

As the result of a Year 2000 problem, a PES may simply stop working, and so is no longer able to perform its normal operation. The nature of Year 2000 problems is such that there is often little prospect of bringing the PES back on-line quickly and continued operation of plant or machine may not be possible.

Impact on Other Control Systems

Safety-related PES are rarely used as the sole means of preventing a hazardous event. They generally work in conjunction with other control systems, and may have backup systems which provide the same level of safety as the main systems. However, it is possible that any PES backup system will fail, (probably simultaneously) as a result of a Year 2000 problem. The effect of this will be that there will be an increased risk of a hazardous event occurring.

Linked Systems

Most systems do not perform in isolation. We need to include the possibility that inputs to the PES being considered (e.g., from another PES or PE device) are erroneous or missing because of Year 2000 problems, and assess the resulting impact on safety. We need also to consider the outputs from the PES being assessed - if there is a possibility that they are incorrect because of a Year 2000 problem, will this affect another PES, which in turn will have an impact on safety?

Impact on Safety and Existing Safety Assessments

Finally we must decide if the failure of PES has a direct or indirect effect on safety, none at all, or whether any existing assessment of the safety of a process or operation is affected by failure due to Year 2000 problems. In many circumstances, failure of a PES resulting from Year 2000 problems will mean that a similar back-up system or replacement component will be subject to the same mode of failure as the PES itself.

This is because Year 2000 problems result from faults which are "systematic" (i.e., faults "built into" the design), and not the random failure of hardware components that are usually experienced. Therefore, all identical components or PES will exhibit the same mode of failure. Replacing a component with a spare is unlikely to effect a satisfactory repair.

More disconcertingly, perhaps, work recently undertaken in Year 2000 investigations shows that systems or components previously thought to be identical need not, in fact, be the same. Manufacturers continually improve/upgrade products and minor components within those products change. These minor components may include the microprocessor, clock or operating system. This raises the prospect that, at the Year 2000, items previously believed to be identical may exhibit different behaviour, i.e., they may fail identically or fail in different ways; some may fail while others do not. Many safety assessments are based on the normally-valid assumption that backup PES or spares will act identically to the units they replace, and so these assumptions now need to be reviewed.

Safety may also be compromised by the failure of planned maintenance and calibration scheduling systems. These systems are clearly date-dependent, and could be prone to error at the Year 2000.

Most safety assessments assume a range of utilities or services which are considered non-vulnerable, such as telephone and FAX communications, water, gas, electricity, ventilation, etc. From the evidence at present, we should anticipate that the major utility providers will continue to successfully provide services through the Year 2000 changeover, but local facilities will need to be re-examined, such as local telephone networks, back-up generators, boiler plant, ventilation systems, and so on. They may be subject to Year 2000 failures, with consequential impact on safety.

3.7 ASSESSING THE FUNCTIONALITY OF PES

When assessing functionality, we need to search for evidence that the PES has built-in date dependencies. The likelihood of failure increases if the PES has functionality which appears to be time-related.

It is not feasible to provide an exhaustive list of all time-related functions which a real-time or embedded system could perform, but the potential for failure increases if a PES does any of the following:-

- displays a date or time;

- implements a timed control sequence;

- performs operations on a timed basis;

- produces hourly/daily/weekly/monthly reports;

- calculates any time-based totals, averages, rates or trends;

- time stamps data, or uses time-stamped data;

- maintains historical data;

- handles timed alarms and events;

- generates alerts at pre-determined times (e.g., planned maintenance or calibration).

3.8 ASSESSING THE CONSTRUCTION OF PES

When reviewing and assessing construction of a system, we need to look at the building blocks of the PES and the way in which they are linked. The likelihood of failure increases if the PES:-

- uses clock or operating system components known to fail;

- uses packages or tools which are not Year 2000 compliant;

- requires entry of date and time on start-up;

- has rolling database files (i.e., delete oldest entry when new one added);

- receives external time signals for synchronisation purposes;

- receives external geographic/positioning data.

3.9 OVERALL VULNERABILITY ASSESSMENT - DECISION SEQUENCE AND CHECKLISTS

So the overall vulnerability of a PES to Year 2000 failure is some combination of its criticality, its functionality and its construction. The likelihood of failure of the PES is primarily determined by the assessment of functionality and construction. The decision as to whether or not such a failure is important in safety terms is based on the criticality assessment. There is no precise measure of vulnerability of a PES, and so the overall assessment of vulnerability is necessarily based on subjective judgement. One method is outlined below.

The overall aim of a vulnerability assessment is to identify the PES which require priority attention in order to ensure safety. A suitable approach is to score the criticality, functionality and construction of each PES on a scale of 0 to 6 (0 representing a low score, and 6 a high score). The scoring should be undertaken by a team to ensure consistency, and previous scorings may need to be revised as new PES are assessed, again to ensure consistency.

The following decision sequence and checklists provide both a mechanism for scoring the assessment criteria of criticality, functionality and construction, and a detailed list of topics to review when investigating potential Year 2000 date dependence problems.

The checklists are designed to give a visual indication of risk level in each case. High risk in the scoring column is always to the left, with low risk to the right. If the checklists are completed using a highlighter or marker pen, then a rapid qualitative assessment of the overall score can be made by reviewing where the balance of the marked scores fall (i.e., when the majority of scores lie to the left, the PES carries a high risk and corresponding high score of failure). Similarly, if very few questions can be answered, the overall score should be high.

In order to complete the decision sequence and checklists, a range of skills are required, which can be summarised as follows:

Criticality - knowledge of the way the PES works, what it produces, and how it interacts with other systems (PES and non-PES);

- appreciation of the requirements for safe operation of the PES and any specific safety regulations covering that part of the process.

Functionality	-	knowledge of the original PES requirements;
	-	knowledge of the way the PES is used and <u>can</u> be used (i.e., capabilities designed into the PES which may currently be unused);
	-	appreciation of the ways in which the PES exchanges information with other systems (PES and non-PES).
Construction	-	ability to determine if a PES contains clock or date dependent components, and whether or not they are in use;
	-	knowledge of the detailed construction of each PES component (in many cases this may only reside with the supplier/manufacturer/maintainer - the checklist in these cases can form the basis of questions to ask of suppliers, etc.).

Of these skill sets, the ability to assess construction is the one least likely to exist within an organisation (especially a small business). In terms of prioritising an investigation, it may not be necessary to answer these questions, at least initially, if the functionality has already indicated a high degree of date dependence.

The questions are, by their nature, technical in scope and do require knowledge of the nature and construction of processor based equipment.

Remember that, at this stage, the aim is to assess the risk and, therefore, 'unknown' is a valid (if high risk) answer. Hopefully, communication with equipment manufacturers will reduce the number of 'unknown' answers to an acceptable level by the time appropriate remedial action has to be considered. The construction checklist should form the basis of detailed questions to be considered by suppliers/manufacturers when assessing compliance.

Some PES components may be so simple as to require only a small number of the overall answers (e.g., simple microcontrollers or smart sensors). In the case where no further answers are necessary in a section of the checklist, the user is prompted to move to the next appropriate section.

The results of the checklists initially are used to provide guidance as to the number of PES which are vulnerable to potential failures, and to assess the priority which should be given to further investigation into the nature and impact of failure and any remedial action required.

In summary, the overall vulnerability of a PES is assessed in three parts:

PART 1 - Assessing Criticality
This is achieved using the decision sequence given in Figure 2, and taking into account the consequences of a safety-related failure.

PART 2 - Assessing Functionality
This is achieved using Checklist 2, which records the date and time functionality of the PES.

PART 3 - Assessing Construction
This is achieved using Checklist 3, which records the likelihood of failure of the components of the PES. Checklist 3 is derived from the results of Checklists 3A to 3D, which record the characteristics of the PES components in detail.

The results of these assessments are then used in the **overall PES vulnerability mapping process**, described in Sections 3.10 and 3.11.

PES VULNERABILITY ASSESSMENT - PART 1
ASSESSING CRITICALITY

There are 2 parameters that should be considered in determining the overall importance to safety of safety-related systems (i.e., its criticality). These are:

a) **Contribution** - this is a measure of the safety purpose of the PES architecture/configuration, and the overall system's immunity to failure (any failure);

b) **Consequence** - this is a measure of the result of failure (i.e., the effect of the hazardous event).

The **Contribution** is obtained from a Decision Sequence as given below:

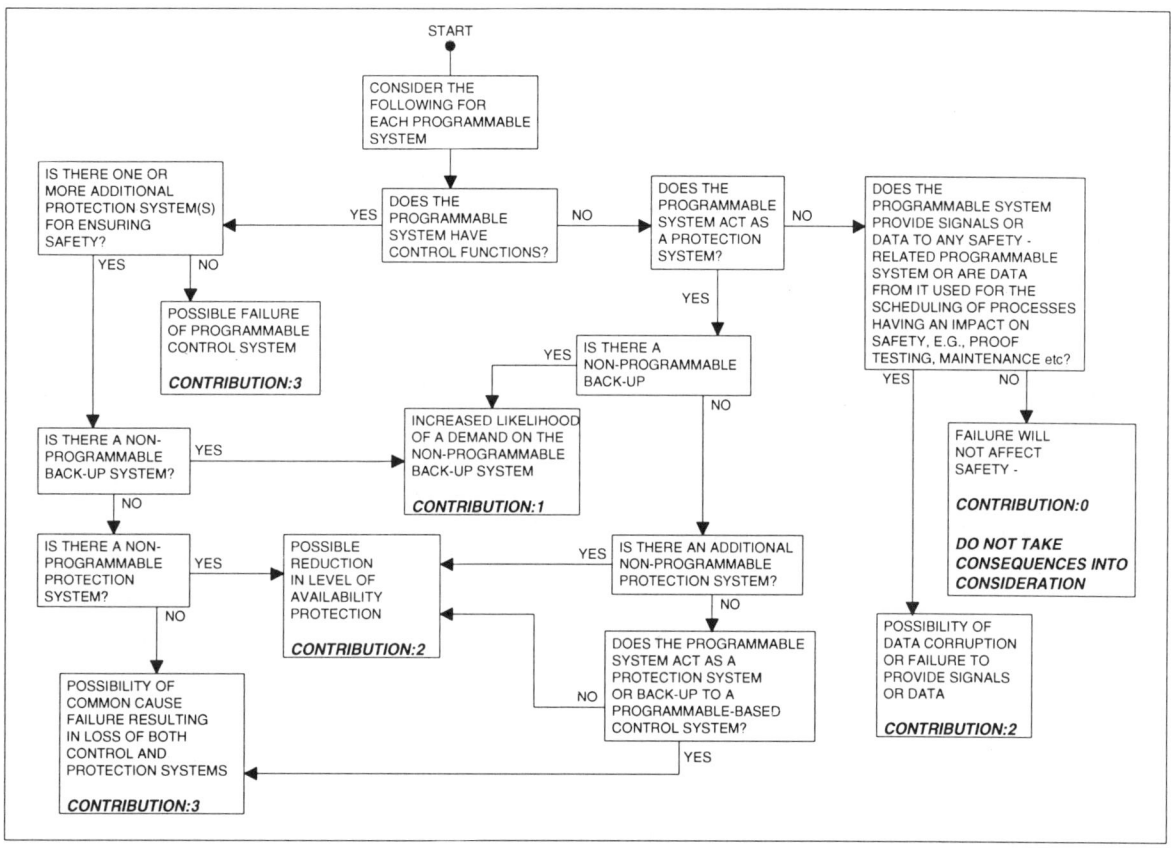

Figure 2
Contribution Decision Sequence

Note that figure 2 is intended only as an aid to developing the prioritisation with respect of safety criticality. It assumes that the risk reduction is spread evenly across all the safety-related systems. The exception to this is with back-up systems, which, for the purposes of Figure 2, are assumed to provide full risk reduction in their own right. In situations where the actual risk reduction is known, a more refined prioritisation may be more appropriate.

The **consequence** is related to effects of the hazardous event, as follows:
No injury = 0
Minor accident / reversible injury = 1
Irreversible injury / loss of one life = 2
Loss of many lives = 3

Overall Criticality Rating (= Contribution + Consequence)   ☐ (0 to 6)

PES VULNERABILITY ASSESSMENT - PART 2
ASSESSING FUNCTIONALITY

Checklist 2 - Functionality

REFER TO PARA	ITEM	OCCURRENCE LEVEL			COMMENTS
	Functionality - Does the PES..				
F1	• display or print a date or time	2	1	0	
F2	• implement a timed control sequence	2	1	0	
F3	• perform operations on a timed basis	2	1	0	
F4	• produce timed reports (hourly/daily/weekly, etc.)	2	1	0	
F5	• calculate time-based totals, averages, rates or trends	2	1	0	
F6	• time-stamp its data, or use time-stamped data	2	1	0	
F7	• maintain historical records	2	1	0	
F8	• display or print data by time sequence	2	1	0	
F9	• generate alerts at pre-determined intervals, e.g., calibration.	2	1	0	
F10	• request the date on start up or allow user entry of date	2	1	0	
F11	• know which day of the week it is by date	2	1	0	
F12	• send or receive date and time information to and from other systems	2	1	0	
F13	• have date-based calibration/maintenance facilities	2	1	0	

Overall Functionality Rating   ☐ (0 to 6)

Functionality Reference Guide

Occurrence Levels: 0 = None
　　　　　　　　　1 = Few/infrequently
　　　　　　　　　2 = Many/frequently

F1 Visible output of the date is a certain indication of date functionality. A 2 digit year increases the chance of failure due to date comparison.

F2 Some timed control sequences are based on absolute calendar operation not just on elapsed time. Such systems are at risk of failure.

F3 Starting or finishing a sequence of actions on a date/time based schedule is a certain indication of date dependence.

F4 Any report whether printed, displayed or stored which contains a date indicates date dependence.

F5 Any calculation that uses an absolute date to calculate a rate, average or trend will use some degree of date arithmetic. This places it at risk of failure.

F6 Data stored by a system or products physically dated by it, indicates date dependency. Use of time-stamped data from electronic tabs, bar-code look up tables or optical character recognition similarly indicates date dependence.

F7 Where a system stores data histories, storage efficiency is often maintained by date/time data vectoring techniques. These use date arithmetic to store only changed data by tagging them with their time of measurement.

F8 Lists of data such as alarms or timed events are often displayed or printed in date order (e.g. newest first). In order to generate such a list, date arithmetic is used.

F9 Some systems include monitoring/diagnostic functionality designed to warn the user when a set running period has been exceeded in order to allow regularly required maintenance to be carried out or because the system has a safe maximum run time. Although in many cases simple elapsed time indicators can carry out these functions, in some instances real-time clock/calendar system is used with associated date arithmetic.

F10 Some systems, which contain only a software clock, will request the time and date when started up or powered on and contain facilities to enter the date and time (e.g., for BST/GMT changes).

F11 Knowledge of the date (or at least the number of the day in the month) and the day of the week implies that some form of calendar functionality exists.

F12 If other systems remain in synchronism with this one or update their date/time when this one is adjusted, then there is a high probability that date/time synchronisation is being carried out by a data connection.

F13 Many systems require regular scheduled maintenance to continue to operate in a safe manner. Where maintenance scheduling is prompted by in-built diagnostics or scheduled by monitoring equipment, a Year 2000 problem in that equipment can mean that maintenance does not occur when required. Failure of a diagnostic system can also prevent essential equipment from operation.

PES VULNERABILITY ASSESSMENT - PART 3
ASSESSING CONSTRUCTION

Checklist 3 - Construction

For very simple PES it may be possible to assess the likelihood of failure based on construction categories directly (at least in some categories). Generally though, this checklist should be addressed by completing the detailed checklists that follow this one to provide an overall likelihood of failure for each of the 4 categories below. For more complex PES it may be necessary to complete the detailed checklists for each component PE. In this case, the overall construction rating should be derived from the checklists for each PE.

REFER TO PARA	ITEM Construction - Assess	LIKELIHOOD OF FAILURE	COMMENTS
CO1	• Clock Mechanisms	6 | 5 | 4 | 3 | 2 | 1 | 0	
CO2	• Operating Systems/Controlling Firmware	6 | 5 | 4 | 3 | 2 | 1 | 0	
CO3	• Programming Support Tools	6 | 5 | 4 | 3 | 2 | 1 | 0	
CO4	• Application Software	6 | 5 | 4 | 3 | 2 | 1 | 0	

Overall Construction Rating ☐ (0 to 6)

Construction Reference Guide

Likelihood of failure
  6=high
  0=low

CO1　Many systems contain clock mechanisms (hardware and/or software) which maintain the date via a stored calendar. Identification of the nature and variety of these clock mechanisms can allow a likelihood of failure to be assessed. See Checklist 3A.

CO2　Most processor systems have either some controlling firmware or software based operating system that carry out their basic functions. This system will generally be common across a variety of models (or even makes) of the system, although may exist in different version or release levels. In assessing likelihood of failure it is important to determine how much of the date functionality of a system resides at this level, even though that functionality may not be apparently used. See Checklist 3B.

CO3　Where a system can be programmed or tailored by the customer, a set of programming support tools may be supplied. They can be as simple as a text editor for a configuration file or a PC-based program to load initialisation or set-point data into the data port of a controller. They can also be as complex as software language compilers and support libraries for PCs or mini-computers or ladder logic generation packages for PLCs. Knowledge of whether these support tools carry out date manipulation and arithmetic is necessary to assess the likelihood of failure. See Checklist 3C.

CO4　Application software is the series of instructions or data which tailors a system to the desired functionality. This is where each system can differ from others of the same make and model and where direct date manipulation can be carried out by a variety of different programmers and techniques. If nothing is known about the actual application code in use, then a system's compliance can only be assessed by testing and even the act of testing can cause the system to fail. See Checklist 3D.

PE VULNERABILITY ASSESSMENT - PART 3A

Checklist 3A - Construction: Clock Mechanisms

REFER TO PARA	ITEM	Y = YES N = NO U = UNKNOWN NA = NOT APPLICABLE LIKELIHOOD OF FAILURE ←HIGH LOW→	COMMENTS
	Clock Mechanisms		
CL1	• Are all clock components identified (e.g. via circuit diagrams, reference guides)	N | U | | Y	
CL2	• Does the system contain a hardware Time of Day (TOD) clock (if NO go to CL10)	Y | U | | N	
CL3	• Does the system maintain the date/time when the power is off (usually via battery or in non-volatile RAM	U | Y | N | NA	
CL4	• Is the year maintained as:- 2 digits [2] 4 digits [4] relative offset [RO]	2 | U | RO | 4	
CL5	• Are sufficient bits assigned to the year to give a reasonable life expectancy (e.g. 2010) from the base date	N | U | Y | NA	
CL6	• Does the TOD clock roll over to 2000 while the system is powered down (Many PC BIOSs fail this test)	N | U | Y | NA	
CL7	• Does the system use a century bit	Y | U | N | NA	
CL8	• Do all system time accesses come from the hardware clock	N | U | Y | NA	
CL9	• Does the system transfer the date to a software clock: on power-up/boot [PU] on a regular basis [R] on change [CH]	R | CH | PU | NA	
CL10	• Is a software clock in use (if NO go to CL14)	Y | U | | N	
CL11	• If a software clock is In use, does it reflect changes back to a hardware TOD clock	N | U | Y | NA	
CL12	• Does the software clock roll-over in a compliant manner	N | U | Y | NA	
CL13	• Does the software clock set appropriate century bits	N | U | Y | NA	
CL14	• Does the system use an external time source: Continuously [CO] on power-up/boot [PU] on change [CH]	CO | CH | PU | NA	

Clock Mechanisms Reference Guide

When reviewing clock mechanisms, it should be remembered that all processors have a clock which is used to determine instruction and memory cycle times. This is not what we are looking for. The clock mechanisms being searched for are those capable of storing and calculating calendar dates.

CL1 In many embedded systems (e.g., PLCs, microcontrollers) it is often necessary to identify clock components (hardware and software) by reference to manufacturer's data sheets or, usually as a last resort, circuit diagrams.

CL2 All PCs, most Single Board Computers and mini-computers will have a TOD clock.

Embedded controllers, such as PLCs, may only have a Time of Day (TOD) clock or registers to hold the date and time as an option. Some maintain TOD as an add-on hardware option. In many cases the model number will vary slightly where TOD hardware processing is present (e.g., 311 doesn't, 331 does).

CL3 Many systems maintain the time and date even when the power is removed. This is sometimes by means of a battery (either re-chargeable or long-life) or on some non-volatile storage mechanism (e.g., NVRAM, bubble memory).

If the system asks you to set the time and date on start-up then it probably does not retain date and time across a power down.

CL4 Date is usually maintained as either a 2 or 4 digit number or a relative offset (e.g., seconds since 1966). 2 digit year storage cannot differentiate 1900 from 2000 and can lead, at least, to leap year related problems. In hardware terms relative offset systems may appear to be the most secure, but in reality usually pass the problem of date evaluation on to system software.

The structure of the year storage can usually be determined from the hardware set-up mechanisms (which may be mechanical (e.g., thumb-wheels), electrical (e.g., push-buttons), or firmware (e.g., BIOS set-up program)).

CL5 This question can generally only be answered by reference to the manufacturer or a technical reference manual. A specific field width in bits may be assigned to store the date (e.g., in a PLC register). The number of bits will determine the range of dates possible (e.g., 4 bits for a year field will give a range of 15 years, 32 bits in seconds will give a range of over 130 years).

CL6 It is common to find that, although an operating system or software component can correctly handle the century change, the simpler code in the firmware or BIOS which deals with it while the power is off generates an incorrect result on a century or leap year roll-over.

CL7 The reason many PC BIOS systems fail to roll over to 2000 when powered off, is that the firmware handling the date calculation fails to set the 'century' bit which tells the operating system (e.g., DOS) that it is in a new century.

CL8 If the operating system/software is constrained to always provide the time/date from the hardware clock, then the possibility of erroneous date calculation is reduced.

CL9 Once again this may need reference to the manufacturer or a technical manual. The risk to the ongoing operation of a system is less if time/date information is only transferred at start-up as the software can be tested in isolation and will contain its own roll-over mechanisms.

CL10 Some systems maintain the time and date by means of software rather than or in addition to special hardware.

CL11 A system can often survive the century change if the new date is transferred back to the hardware clock (e.g., DOS 5 and 6 will handle the change where a BIOS may not).

CL12 It is necessary to carry out date checks on both hardware and software components of any clock mechanism as they will usually handle date storage and calculation in different ways.

CL13 If a hardware century bit exists, it is necessary to ensure that it has been set by both hardware and software (i.e., powered on and powered off).

CL14 If the system is synchronised to an external time-source (e.g., master computer, Rugby clock, GPS) on a continuous or change basis then the likelihood of failure becomes more difficult to assess, as it is dependent on both the external source providing the correct date and the system interpreting it correctly. These systems are also much harder to test, as simulation of the remote time signal is usually necessary. If the system is only synchronised at start-up, then at least the ability to roll over to the new century is purely internal (although it may have problems on a later synchronisation).

PE VULNERABILITY ASSESSMENT - PART 3B

Checklist 3B - Construction: Operating System/Controlling Firmware

REFER TO PARA	ITEM	Y = YES N = NO U = UNKNOWN NA = NOT APPLICABLE LIKELIHOOD OF FAILURE ←HIGH LOW →	COMMENTS
OS1	**Operating System and Controlling Firmware** • Does the system contain controlling firmware which allows date/time adjustment (if NO go to (OS3)	Y | U | | N	
OS2	• Do all spares use the same revisions	N | U | Y | NA	
OS3	• Is there a separately identified operating system present (if NO go to OS7)	Y | U | | N	
OS4	• Are the operating system/control firmware date dependencies known/documented	N | U | Y | NA	
OS5	• Is the interface between operating system and firmware defined	N | U | Y | NA	
OS6	• Does the operating system provide time/date interrogation and calculation facilities as standard	N | U | Y | NA	
OS7	• Does the system produce or rely on data files (if NO go to next checklist)	Y | U | | N	

OS8	• Does the file system maintain the date of individual files as:
	    relative offset [RO]
	    binary absolute [BA]
	    ASCII absolute [AA]
	    part of file name [F]
		F | AA | BA | RO	

OS9	• Does the operating system use file management features like:
	    date based back-up
	    date validation
	    deletion/compaction by date
	    removal of 'old' versions
		Y | U | N | NA	

OS10	• Does file management store:
	    creation date
	    last accessed date
	    last modified date
	    file audit trails
	    multiple versions by date
		Y | U | N | NA	

Operating System and Controlling Firmware Reference Guide

OS1   There is usually a high degree of interdependence between an operating system and code contained on a motherboard or CPU card (controlling firmware). This code is generally designed to provide an ability to start-up the system software, contain controlling data relating to hardware and peripherals, and, frequently, to maintain the system time and date. The complexity of this code can vary from simple hard-coded instructions to fully interactive virtual console or menuing systems.

System date dependencies may reside in the operating system and/or the controlling firmware. In order to inspect or test a system, it is necessary to know where and in what way dates are handled.

OS2 Where spares of motherboards, SBCs, CPU cards or complete microcontrollers are carried, any testing or inspection carried out on the system can be invalidated by the use of a spare with a different firmware revision.

OS3 Simpler devices may have no visible operating system at all. In this case the opportunity for mis-match of hardware and software in terms of differently handling dates is removed.

OS4 The use of dates in the operating system and controlling firmware can often be found in the User's Guide or Technical Reference Manual.

OS5 It is necessary to be aware of the level of interaction between any operating system and the controlling firmware and how date information is exchanged between them. In very simple microcontroller systems the interaction may be directly between the controlling firmware and the application code.

OS6 Systems where the operating system provides standard mechanisms for date/time manipulation and calculation are simpler to verify for compliance than those where all such work is carried out in the application software (i.e., at the mercy of individual programmers).

OS7 If a system produces or relies on the contents of data files, then some organised form of storage will be used (whether on disk or memory devices). In most cases date and time information will be stored along with the files or even individual data records.

OS8 If the system stores time-stamped data-files or data records (possibly in a database), then the possibility of date manipulation errors occurring increases with the level of storage (e.g., determining which is the latest file is a simple subtraction where date/time is stored as a relative offset, interpreting an ASCII date or extracting data from a filename requires a significantly more complex algorithm).

OS9 Many operating systems provide file management features designed to keep a system safe or to ensure efficient use of a storage system. Ironically, these can introduce complex date based algorithms into the day to day running of the system and hence increase the possibility of a date dependent problem.

OS10 File management systems can store the date in a number of ways for every file or even data element handled. It is important that each of the mechanisms used is carefully reviewed.

PE VULNERABILITY ASSESSMENT - PART 3C

Checklist 3C - Construction: Programming Support Tools

REFER TO PARA	ITEM	Y = YES N = NO U = UNKNOWN NA = NOT APPLICABLE LIKELIHOOD OF FAILURE ←HIGH LOW →	COMMENTS
	Programming Support Tools		
PST1	• Are programming support tools supplied with the system (if NO go to next check-list)	Y U N	
PST2	• Does the operating-system supply standard date/time routines for all Programming Support Tools to use	N U Y NA	
PST3	• Do any Programming Support Tools have their own date manipulation routines	Y U N NA	
PST4	• Are any automatic 'tidy up' mechanisms date related (e.g. database tidy up)	Y U N NA	
PST5	• Are rate calculation routines present which use a time/date difference basis	Y U N NA	
PST6	• Are automatic audit trails (time-stamped) generated	Y U N NA	
PST7	• Are data histories maintained	Y U N NA	

Programming Support Tools Reference Guide

PST1   Programming Support Tools increase the likelihood of failure because they provide the means to amend a system, and so it becomes non-standard. Where application software is generated using standard facilities such as SCADA or Graphics packages, mathematical, statistical or data manipulation libraries or ladder logic generation, automatic build or diagnostic tools, it is necessary to review the date dependent elements of these before assessing the application software. Remember that even if the facilities are not used currently, future modifications to the system may cause date dependent errors to appear if unchecked facilities are used.

PST2   Facilities which make use of operating system date routines are generally more robust than those which contain their own date manipulation facilities. Unfortunately, where such facilities exist to make code 'portable', internal handling of date data is usually the case (e.g., even where an absolute date is available from a system, C based libraries will normally convert it back to the UNIX standard relative offset).

PST3   A search should be made of available documentation to determine if any date manipulation or date dependent facilities are provided by standard support packages.

PST4   Just as with file management facilities, any 'tidy up' mechanisms hidden in support libraries or packages are a source of potential date-related failures.

PST5   Any routines used for providing time differences from two absolute dates are an area of potential failure.

PST6   Where packages provide audit trails of date stamped actions, a failure potential exists either during the generation of such records or the re-application of them during a recovery process.

PST7   Where systems capture regular real-time data, historical records of changes in that data are often stored using a date/time vectoring technique.

PE VULNERABILITY ASSESSMENT - PART 3D

Checklist 3D - Construction: Application Software

REFER TO PARA	ITEM	Y = YES N = NO U = UNKNOWN NA = NOT APPLICABLE LIKELIHOOD OF FAILURE ←HIGH LOW→	COMMENTS
	Application Software		
AS1	• Is any information available on the application software (if NO - finished)	N Y	
AS2	• Is the functionality of the software well understood	N U Y NA	
AS3	• Is the design of the software well documented	N U Y NA	
AS4	• Does the software generally behave reliably	N U Y NA	
AS5	• Are the sources available	N U Y NA	
AS6	• Are the development facilities compliant	N U Y NA	
AS7	• Does the design insist on use of standard libraries for date handling	N U Y NA	
AS8	• Is configuration control maintained	N U Y NA	
AS9	• Is there confidence that the software can be migrated to a new operating system/hardware platform	N U Y NA	
AS10	• Does the supplier still exist	N U Y NA	
AS11	• Is there a current maintenance agreement	N U Y NA	
AS12	• Are the original acceptance tests available	N U Y NA	
AS13	• Does the system use: Fixed Code [F] e.g. Compiled code/ Ladder logic Interpreted code User changeable code [UC] e.g. Ladder logic (soft), Co-processor software, Script files, Macros, Initialisation/configuration files	UC U F NA	
AS14	• Does the system use: SCADA libraries Graphics libraries Maths libraries	N U Y NA	

Application Software Reference Guide

AS1   All processor based systems (i.e., capable of utilising a real-time clock) will contain some elements of application software even in the form of a set of instructions used to configure or tailor the system to your set-up (e.g., ladder logic in a PLC, set-points in a microcontroller).

The potential for failure with application software generally relates to the level of knowledge of any date handling which might occur. Assessment in this case is a matter of looking for clues of date activity. Testing of a complex package via a mock millennium change may provide a go/no-go result but will probably not trigger all date facilities unless the test itself is created from an in-depth knowledge of the software functionality.

AS2 If little knowledge is available of the detailed functionality of the software, then the opportunities for evaluating date dependencies are reduced and the possibility of failing to detect potential failure areas increased. In most cases this level of knowledge is only available from the original designers/authors of the software. This may not necessarily be the suppliers.

AS3 If the software design is not well documented (e.g., high degree of on-site development/modification) then determining date dependencies can be very much a hit-or-miss affair.

AS4 If the software does not behave in a robust manner (i.e., fails regularly, needs frequent reboot or restart) then any additional failure such as a failed date calculation is much more likely to cause problems.

AS5 Lack of access to the sources means that standard date search mechanisms (automatic or manual) cannot be applied.

AS6 It should be remembered that in the case of software (or even firmware) dependent systems, the development facilities may also suffer from date dependencies (e.g., automated ladder logic generators for PLCs, build routines for microcontrollers, portable load/diagnostic devices).

AS7 If standard libraries are used then the variations in date handling are restricted to those libraries and not the creativity of individual programmers.

AS8 If the changes to the application software are not well controlled then additional failure potential will be incurred.

AS9 In many cases, the application software may be compliant but the platform it is running on may not. In this case the remedy will be to re-host the software on a new hardware or operating system platform.

AS10 Lack of access to the original authors/supplier greatly increases the possibility of not being able to detect and remedy problems.

AS11 The evaluation and upgrade of application software covered by a maintenance agreement would normally infer that a reasonable level of in-depth knowledge relating to functionality and design exists, thereby reducing the likelihood of failure not being detected or remedied.

AS12 Once a remedy has been applied it may be necessary to carry out regression testing to determine that the changes have not impacted on some other area of the software functionality. The availability of the original acceptance tests reduces this risk.

AS13 The ability of general users to modify the code or operating parameters of a system increases the possibility that date dependencies can be introduced. This may be as innocuous as a configuration control text file (e.g. start this run on 02/02/00) or an automatically updated initialisation file.

AS14 The use of libraries to carry out standard functions reduces the possibility of programmer or user introduced date dependencies.

3.10 OVERALL SYSTEM VULNERABILITY MAPPING

The purpose of this section is to develop an overall system vulnerability map using the assessments done in section 3.9.

The simple summation or multiplication of the scores (derived from parts 1 - 3 of the vulnerability assessment) to provide an overall score for the system is not recommended, as the result can mask some important information. Instead, a useful mechanism to adopt is a map of the style shown in Figure 3. Here a number of PES are plotted on axes representing Functionality and Construction, whereas the Criticality of the PES is represented by the diameter of the circle.

The PES in **Quadrant 1** are not only critical to safety, but have also been assessed to have functional and construction characteristics which imply a high likelihood of failure.

The PES which appear in **Quadrant 2** are less functional, but their construction characteristics suggest they are vulnerable. The solutions will probably involve replacing hardware or package components with Year 2000-compliant equivalents. If this is not feasible, whole system replacement may be necessary.

Quadrant 3 is where we expect to find many simple embedded systems – they are not highly functional, and do not contain too many complex construction elements. However, these systems should be carefully considered as they are nonetheless prone to failure, and the major determinant here should be the criticality rating (i.e., the size of the circle).

The systems in **Quadrant 4** have considerable date-dependent functionality, but are likely to be soundly constructed and probably use components which are Year 2000 compliant. This means that the investigation can concentrate on the way in which the application software has been constructed. Most solutions will involve updating software, rather than replacing whole systems.

As an example, in the map shown in Figure 3, the system PES1 has a high likelihood of failure because of its functionality and construction, but scores low in terms of criticality. The system PES2 is assessed as being important to safety, but is less likely to fail due to its functionality. System PES3 scores low on all counts, and so is likely to be a low priority.

This approach to vulnerability assessment, and representation via the system vulnerability map, is an approximate but nonetheless swift and powerful method of visualising the characteristics of a range of PES. By prioritising effort based on the vulnerability assessment, individuals and teams tasked with Year 2000 rectification programmes will be able to concentrate on major safety PES issues.

Note also that the vulnerability assessments should not simply be undertaken at the outset of the programme. By their very nature, they are approximations, and as the programme proceeds, better information will come to light. It is essential to recognise that vulnerability assessment is an iterative process. **It should be visited at regular intervals throughout the Year 2000 programme, in order that more precise assessments can be made.** As a result, the rectification programme can be regularly re-planned.

3.11 APPLYING THE RESULTS OF THE VULNERABILITY MAPPING

The aim of the vulnerability map is to provide a basis for developing the priorities of the rectification programme. The overall system vulnerability map is a useful method of identifying the PES with the highest likelihood of failure, and this is important information to take into account when planning the rectification programme. However, in addition to "likelihood of failure", the rectification programme should be developed with two other major criteria in mind:-

- **criticality**: the largest diameter circles represent the PES deemed to be most safety-critical. The rectification programme must give sufficient priority to the fixes for such PES, to ensure that they are scheduled for completion in advance of any date considered likely to affect the PES;

- **time to rectify**: some PES can be fixed and re-deployed very quickly, but others will require considerable development and re-testing time. The rectification team must ensure that PES with a long lead time to fix are scheduled into the programme at a suitably early stage.

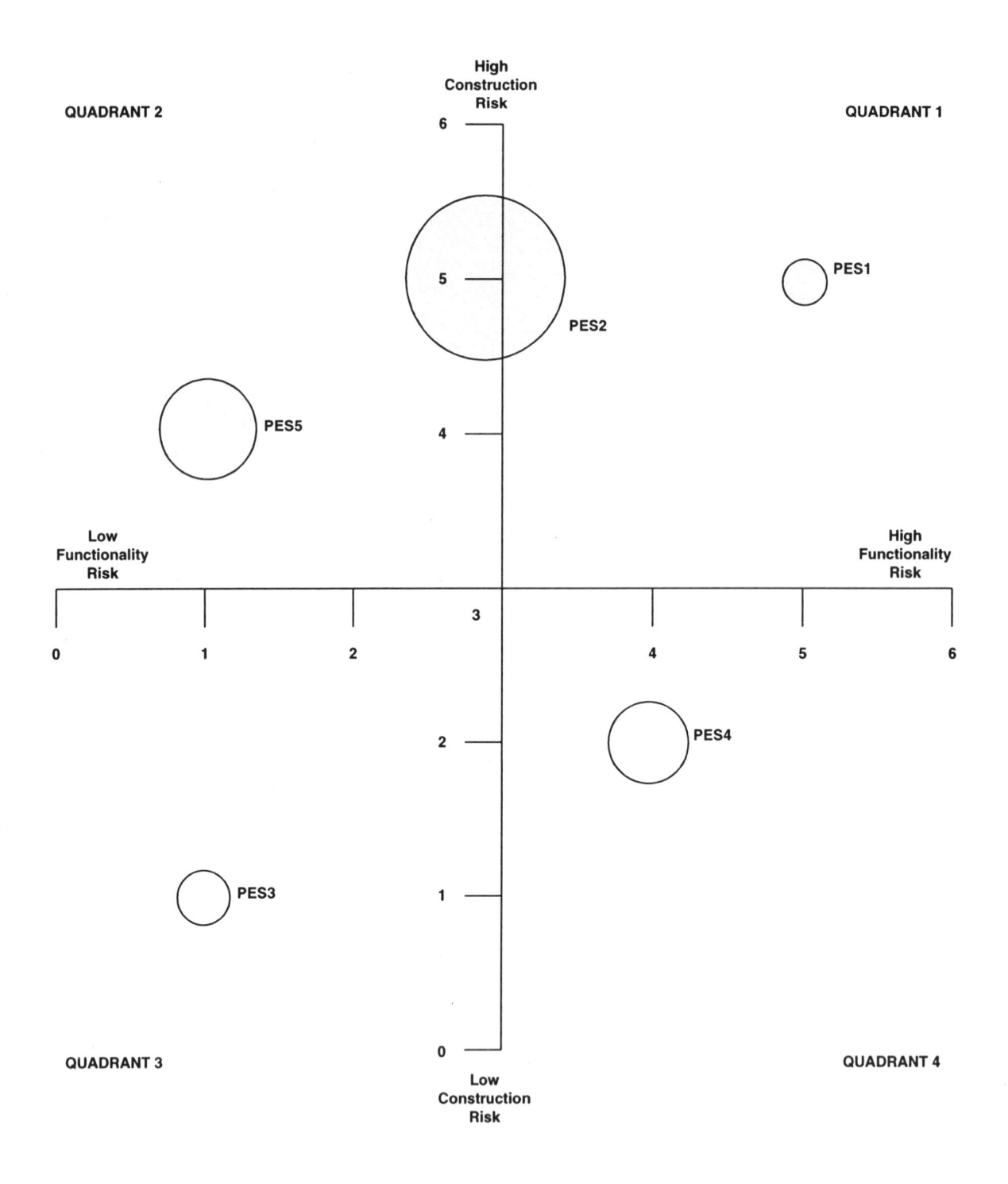

**Figure 3
System Vulnerability Map**

4. APPROACH TO SOLVING THE PROBLEM

4.1 INTRODUCTION

Solving the Year 2000 problem is a project which has a fixed end date. The time available to execute the programme of work decreases continuously. Therefore, priorities, key roles and responsibilities should be defined now.

This section begins by describing the three stage approach to addressing the Year 2000 problem. It then provides details on the roles and responsibilities of key personnel at each of the three stages, and provides guidance on planning and management aspects.

4.2 THE PROGRAMME

The approach to solving the problem should follow the three stage approach in order to secure the most safe (and cost-effective) resolution of the Year 2000 problem. The three stages are:

- Audit and Analysis;
- Strategy and Planning;
- Implementation and Test.

Although there are three distinct stages, it may at times be more prudent to overlap the stages. For example, during the Audit and Analysis Stage, a major PES which has a high criticality rating may be found to be non-compliant. The scale of changes to that PES or the lead time to achieve a compliant PES may mean that the corrective action should be initiated immediately. A sample project plan showing the various tasks in each stage is contained in Figure 4.

Each of the stages is now introduced in this section and described in more detail in the following sections.

4.2.1 Audit and Analysis

The first part of the audit involves IT and system specialists and aims to identify every PES which has a safety impact or carries embedded time-based data. The characteristics of each PES (hardware, operating systems, products, applications languages, etc.) are recorded.

The second part of the audit involves safety, production and business managers and suppliers to determine the impact of the PES on safety (and the production and processes of the business).

Having established this baseline, some of the PES being examined are subjected to triage, which effectively involves assigning degrees of urgency and deciding the order in which they are to be investigated. Selected PES may then be put through a mock millennium change, and their resultant behaviour analysed. With PES where failure could result in a hazardous event, this should not be undertaken, in which case the assessment of the Year 2000 effect requires to be desk-based.

Given the results of the mock millennium change, possible technical solutions for each of the PES are then developed, and the likely cost and safety/production/process impacts are analysed. This stage is completed through the creation of a full report which identifies:-

- whether or not the PES can be referred back to the original suppliers;
- where workarounds are possible, with changes to operating procedures;

- the ease or difficulty of the technical solution;

- whether or not the PES should be replaced rather than attempt a fix;

- the cost/timescale impact of possible solutions. The safety/production/process impact of possible solutions.

4.2.2 Strategy and Planning

The Audit and Analysis Stage provides all of the facts, and the Strategy and Planning Stage is used to make the decisions on how best to address the Year 2000 problem(s). This stage requires close co-operation between staff with different perspectives and knowledge. Through refinement with the IT, engineering and management specialists, a comprehensive strategy (with options where feasible) for the way ahead should be created.

Based on this strategy, a detailed project plan should be created, which will identify the effects on safety, production, equipment, or working practices of each stage of the corrective programme. It will also identify the acceptance criteria which will be applied to each part of the implementation programme.

Working with the safety decision-makers, the team will then agree the details of the Implementation and Testing Stage (see below), and the methods which will be used to undertake the corrective programme.

4.2.3 Implementation and Testing

The Implementation and Testing Stage may have an impact on the safety, operation or revenue-earning capacity of the organisation.

In some PES, the fix required will be relatively simple, although for many, the required amendments could be more complex. In all cases, however, the major task will be in re-testing the system under Year 2000 change conditions. This is the stage at which the impacts on the processes, production and equipment will be most apparent. The programme of re-testing will require to be carried out in a highly-flexible manner, to take account of the continually-changing needs of the business. There will nonetheless come a point with each PES at which the revised version needs to be tested in the real environment, and this will require close co-ordination with the safety and production managers responsible for the operation of the processes and plant.

This final stage is complete when the acceptance criteria have been met by a comprehensive acceptance testing programme.

4.3 PROGRAMME MANAGEMENT

The Programme Manager has a vital role to play in the project. There are several key issues which make programme management more focused and more effective. These include focusing on the programme priorities, which are to:

- maintain safety standards;

- preserve environmental integrity;

- stay in business;

- focus on keeping mission-critical systems functioning;

- minimise revenue loss;

- adopt safety-conscious solutions.

The Programme Manager should ensure that the key issues are addressed and that:

- each part of the programme is realistic and achievable;
- there is high-level education and commitment;
- there is local buy-in and involvement;
- local decisions are made on priorities;
- the programme is audited.

The programme may be the largest single project within an organisation, with potentially greater risk to health and safety than any previous project. It should be managed to ensure that no risks to health and safety are introduced, and that high criticality systems are addressed as early as possible.

Visibility is vital throughout the programme, and this visibility should reach all levels of the company. At a very early stage in the programme, awareness sessions/ seminars should be provided for staff. This will ensure that there is awareness of the subject and will reduce the likelihood of any PES being missed.

At some point, it may be necessary to provide evidence of compliance and work undertaken to ensure compliance. Therefore, all decisions should be recorded and an audit trail maintained. Independent programme audits should be scheduled to take place during the programme.

Management of the programme is a considerable task and the programme manager should ensure adherence to the programme. There is a fixed end date and the level of dependence on third parties is high. Therefore, it is recommended that, allied to the programme/project plan, there is a risk management plan. This is not only a significant management tool, but may also become an important document in any future litigation. In particular, if there were a safety incident at some later date, the risk management plan may be used to show that the company took all reasonably practicable steps to ensure that health and safety issues were fully addressed.

4.4 ROLES AND RESPONSIBILITIES

There are several roles (with associated responsibilities) which should be fulfilled on the Year 2000 Project. For large organisations, each role may be filled by a different person. For small and medium sized organisations, the same person may discharge more than one role, and may even discharge all of the roles. Each of the roles is involved at certain stages of the project as detailed in the responsibility matrix shown in Table 5.

Role	Responsibility
Programme Manager	Ultimately responsible for the success of the Year 2000 project. The programme manager should be a very senior person with authority to make decisions and authorise work. This position requires the full support of the directors of the company.

Project Manager(s)	Responsible for all or part of the Year 2000 project. In a small/medium sized organisation, the project manager may also be the programme manager. In larger organisations, there are often several project managers, each one responsible for a specific area of the project. For example, in a manufacturing organisation, there could be a project manager for IT, one for real-time systems, and one to manage external suppliers (e.g., suppliers of raw material to the production /manufacturing process). Alternatively, in a multi-site organisation, there may be one project manager for each site.
System Specialist(s)	Responsible for assessing the PES for Year 2000 problems, implementation of fixes, and testing and commissioning. The make-up and size of the team of system specialists may vary at different stages of the project. Depending on the level of expertise available within an organisation, this may be an external resource.
Safety Team	Responsible for providing information on the impact which PES have on safety within the workplace and for ensuring that the plant safety assessment is not compromised during or after the Year 2000 project.
Business Manager(s)	Responsible for assessing the impact that any stage of the Year 2000 project may have on the organisational finances.
Production Manager(s)	Responsible for providing information on production schedules, planned shutdowns and assisting to plan how the rectification and test programme can be accommodated within the schedule.
End Users	Responsible for providing information on how PES operate in practice (as opposed to how they were intended to operate). This is a vital input to system assessment.
IT Staff	Responsible for providing information on how IT/production systems interface.
Third Parties	May be responsible for conducting an independent assessment of readiness for Year 2000.

The Year 2000 programme should take precedence over other IT projects. It requires the most experienced and qualified staff, who are experts in their area.

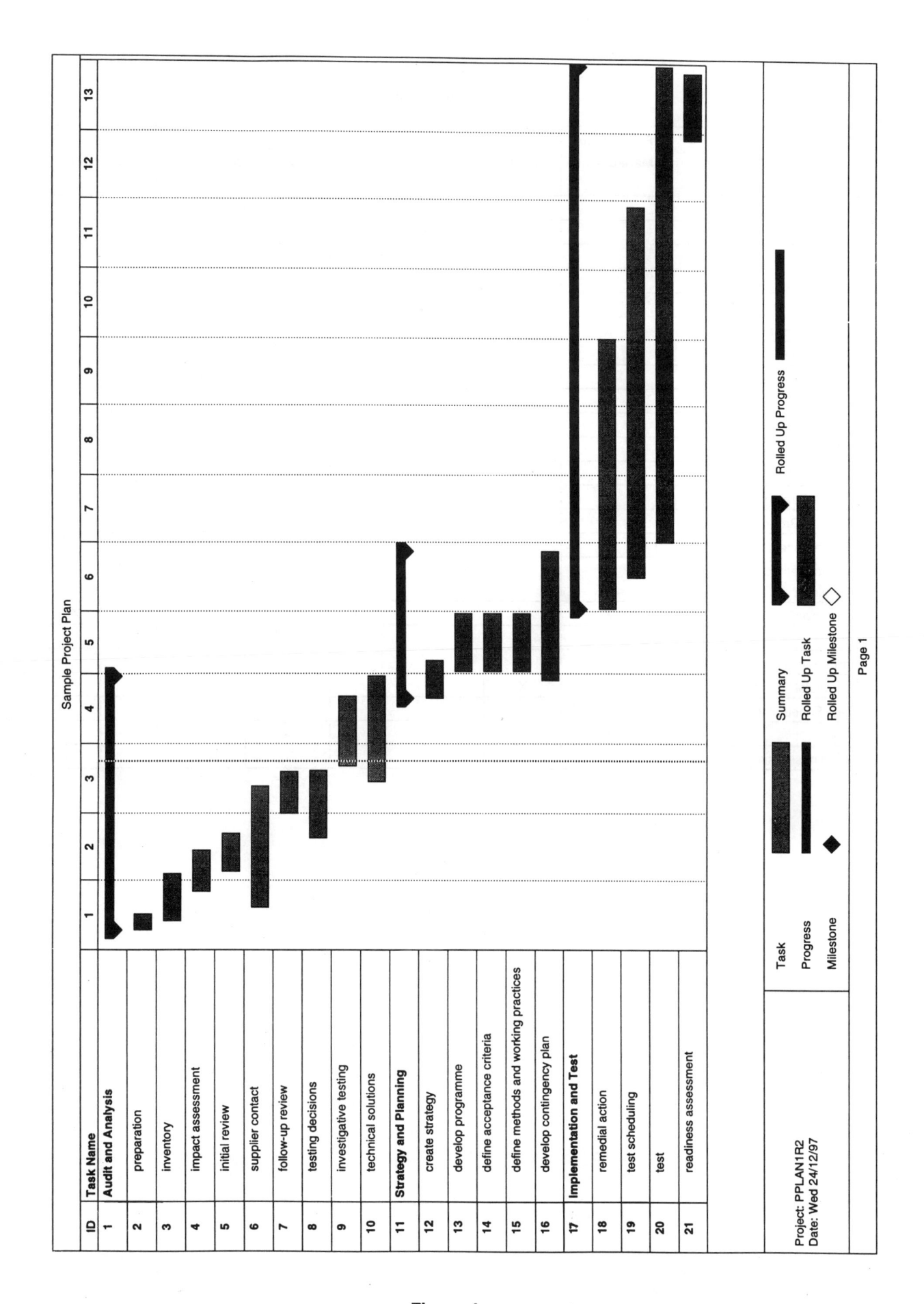

Figure 4
Sample Project Plan

Table 5
Responsibility Matrix

	Programme Manager	Project Manager	Systems Specialist(s)	Safety Team	Business Managers	Production Managers	End Users	IT Staff	Third Parties
Audit & Analysis Stage									
Preparation	X	X	X						
Inventory	X		X			X	X	X	
Impact Assessment	X	X		X	X	X	X		
Initial Review	X		X						
Supplier Contact	X		X						
Follow-Up Review	X		X						
Testing Decisions	X	X	X			X			
Investigative Testing	X		X			X			
Technical Solutions	X	X	X						
Strategy & Planning									
Create Strategy	X	X		X	X	X		X	
Develop Programme	X	X			X	X			
Define Acceptance Criteria	X	X							
Define Methods and Working Practices	X	X							
Develop Contingency Plan	X	X		X	X	X		X	
Implementation & Test									
Remedial Action	X	X	X						
Test Scheduling	X	X	X		X	X			
Test	X	X	X		X	X	X		
Readiness Assessment	X	X	X		X				X

5. AUDIT AND ANALYSIS STAGE

5.1 INTRODUCTION

This section describes the Audit and Analysis Stage of the programme and provides detailed guidance on each of the tasks to be undertaken. This aim of this stage is to determine the scale of the problem within an organisation, the solutions available and the impact (safety, costs) on processes and production.

In common with the overall programme, many tasks may overlap. For example, it is often advantageous to contact suppliers throughout the inventory task. Their advice ("there is no real time clock in this system") can often help to reduce time-consuming activities.

5.2 AUDIT OUTLINE

The audit is a large part of this stage. For planning purposes, an audit of a site which has around 30 systems may typically take 12-14 elapsed weeks. Supplier contact is a time-consuming process, and typically takes 6-8 weeks. Therefore, it is imperative to initiate supplier contact as early as is practical. From the authors' experience, there are a number of problems which are common to many audits, and these are presented in Appendix B.

The audit phase can be broken down into a number of tasks, as follows:

- preparation;

- inventory;

- impact assessment;

- initial review;

- supplier contact;

- follow-up review;

- testing decisions;

- investigative testing **(NB: Testing of a safety-related control PES should not be undertaken if the possible consequences of its failure could result in a hazardous event)**.

Each of these tasks is now described.

5.3 PREPARATION

The starting point of the Audit and Analysis Stage may be an existing system inventory, a system inventory created specifically for the Year 2000 project or no inventory at all. Regardless of the starting point, it is essential that Audit and Analysis is conducted using an accurate system inventory. This means that even if the inventory already exists, it should be validated. In a number of audits carried out by the authors, the inventory validation process has trebled the number of entries in the inventory.

The easiest and most reliable way to validate (or create) an inventory is to walk round the site, but there is some useful preparation before the walkround. Failure to prepare before starting an inventory will mean that items will be missed, often entire systems.

Preparation should include:

a) **Identify the entirety of the site**

   A site layout plan is a useful aid here and should help to highlight:

   - perimeter systems;
   - personnel entry;
   - security systems;
   - restricted access areas;
   - fire alarm/protection;
   - remote areas of the plant.

It is also worth considering parts of the site that may not be the responsibility of one organisation, e.g., a nitrogen production facility which is on-site but is run by a separate organisation may be essential to operation of the plant.

b) **Generate an investigation plan**

   From the information obtained above, generate an investigation plan which includes:

   - the areas to be inspected at a site visit;
   - key personnel to meet with (e.g., End Users), remembering that site electricians may be more able to point out PES (particularly embedded systems) than the Production Manager or IT Staff;
   - a programme which is organised to fit into shift rotas and available plant downtime. Some PE devices have interlocked access and it will not be possible to examine the device without a plant shutdown;
   - the physical boundaries of each PES.

5.4 INVENTORY

The inventory should contain every PES that could contain logic, whether it has a safety function, date processing or not.

The information to be recorded in the inventory should include for each PES and its PE components:

- Model number;
- Serial number (if it is simple to identify);
- Function;
- Software/firmware versions;
- End users contact details;
- Addresses and Contacts for suppliers, manufacturers and maintainers;
- Support/warranty position;

- Spares held (which also need to be compliant and may be able to provide a test bed for compliance assessment);

- Development/Diagnostic/Calibration/Portable equipment (a system may appear compliant, but cannot be fault diagnosed or re-programmed due to support system failure).

It is useful to record the inventory as a spreadsheet (or in a database) and use the spreadsheet to track each system through the programme. This will then form the Quality/Audit Record for the programme.

5.4.1 Definition of a System (PES)

A common mistake in creating an inventory is to misunderstand what is meant by a system (PES). The important thing to assess is the compliance of the PES, not merely the compliance of its components. For the purpose of the Year 2000 programme, a PES:

a) is **supplied** from a single source (this identifies responsibility for overall compliance statements and is not always the manufacturer);

b) has a **number of components** (PE) which can be uniquely identified by:

- function;
- model number;
- manufacturer;
- version number.

and each component has an individual compliance

It is important to remember that identical PLCs in a PES will almost certainly have different functions and probably different firmware/logic software. In this case, each PLC, firmware and logic software is a separate component of the PES.

c) has a **failure potential** (i.e., does it contain elements with date retrieval or is constructed of (or with) elements which may fail);

d) has a failure **criticality**;

- safety (as described in section 3);
- environmental effects;
- revenue.

e) can be attributed a **compliance** status. It is possible for a system to be functionally compliant, whilst containing non-compliant components (e.g., a PLC which fails to rollover compliantly may continue to operate compliantly if it does not use the date registers).

5.4.2 Guidance for the Site Walkround

There are a number of issues to consider for the site walkround:

a) unless you are certain a system is <u>not</u> a PES it should be included in the inventory, even though it may appear to be outside the scope. It is easier to discard a PES later on than to revisit the site at a later date, or worse still, ignore the PES totally;

b) talk to the End Users. They are often aware of new PES or changes to existing PES;

c) do not assume that because someone says there isn't a processor in a particular cabinet that they are correct (e.g., even items such as earth leakage detectors may be microprocessor-based). Use knowledge of the plant process to determine whether it is possible that there is a processor;

d) cover every area of the site.

5.5 IMPACT ASSESSMENT

Impact Assessment is concerned with assessing the potential consequences to safety of a Year 2000 failure of each PES. Impact Assessment does not assess the likelihood of a PES having a problem. This means that the functionality and construction aspects which have been discussed in Section 3 do not form part of the Impact Assessment.

Impact Assessment should consider different types of Year 2000 failure and not only a complete failure of a PES. For example, a PES which operates incorrectly may be less safe than a PES which ceases to operate. Various potential failure modes are described in Section 3.

The Impact Assessment should be carried out by a team which includes:

- safety specialists;
- end users;
- production managers (and engineers), familiar with the site;
- business managers.

The assessment should involve detailed consideration of the function, or functions, of each PES in its operational context. It is important that the information and reasoning is retained to be used by specialists carrying out the next stage of the process, and also for the management of any outstanding items. This information can be recorded in the System Vulnerability Assessment.

5.6 INITIAL REVIEW

The Initial Review aims to obtain detailed information on each PES and to carry out an initial assessment of the construction and functionality aspects of vulnerability (see Section 3). The Initial Review should be "read-only" since an over-eager, unprepared Year 2000 test may have a significant impact on safety.

Sources of information for the Initial Review include:

a) warranty/support agreements - these can used to determine compliance levels and the level of response which can be expected from the supplier;

b) documentation - this can provide information on date dependence, e.g., start-up sequences, block diagrams, date range definitions, housekeeping, logs and reports, interactions with other systems.

Interactions with other systems, both PES and non-PES, should be investigated in detail. A system can cause another system to fail by exporting illegal date data, or by receiving legal or illegal date data (e.g., some BIOS-based systems will rollover to 2000 but will not accept it as a year input).

As well as obvious functional components, it is important to consider construction tools, development tools, spares, diagnostic and maintenance systems. Failure to consider these may have a significant safety impact. For example, if the system software is a language which requires to be compiled and linked, both the compiler and linker should be able to function correctly over the Year 2000.

Using the guidance on System Vulnerability Assessment contained in Section 3, the initial assessment of functionality and construction should be completed.

It may be possible to dismiss PES at this stage as not requiring further action. (Refer to Section 3 for guidance on how to determine if a PES falls into this category).

5.7 SUPPLIER CONTACT

Supplier Contact aims to determine whether the supplier <u>believes</u> a PES is compliant. It does not determine the compliance status of a PES, because there is the possibility that a PES claimed by a supplier to be compliant will prove not to be compliant. However, supplier contact does provide useful information and is an important exercise.

Supplier Contact is necessary for suppliers of PES and safety related services. Experience shows that to get the best possible quality of response, it is important to:

a) **Be specific** - Give as much specific detail as possible as to the make and model, and its use in the PES (or process). This will help the supplier to narrow down the area to be investigated.

b) **Be persistent** - As the Year 2000 approaches, suppliers will be extremely busy.

c) **Do not threaten** - This will not encourage co-operation, only legal wrangles. Stress that this is a request for co-operation.

d) **Keep records** - Record all correspondence, written or verbal.

e) **Anticipate delays in responding** - Delays will grow as more companies realise their responsibilities and exposure, and seek information from suppliers.

Figure 6 contains a flowchart which describes the sequence of activities associated with supplier contact. The activities are as follows:

a) **Initial Telephone Contact** - Call the supplier to determine if the supplier has nominated an individual within its organisation to deal specifically with Year 2000 issues relating to its products. Call the nominated person and make them aware that you are dealing with the issue for your organisation. If the supplier no longer exists, see below (unsupported software).

b) **Letter to supplier** - Send a letter to the nominated person in the supplier organisation requesting details of compliance. If there is not a nominated person in the supplier organisation, address the letter to a senior employee. The letter should also give a target response timescale (2 weeks is not unreasonable). Sample letters are contained in Appendix D.

c) **Check supplier has received letter** - Contact the supplier again and check that it has received the letter. If it has not, resend the letter, and use recorded delivery this time. If the supplier has received the letter, confirm that it will be able to respond within the required timescale, and if it cannot, agree a revised timescale.

d) **Check response is imminent** - Between 3 days and a week before the response from the supplier is due, contact the supplier to check that it plans to respond within the required timescale.

e) **Check response** - When the response from the supplier has been received, check to ensure that it is a complete response, and that is has not omitted any key issues. If there are any areas which have not been successfully addressed, re-initiate contact with the supplier. Assessing supplier responses is dealt with in more detail later in this section.

f) **Supplier Visit** - if it seems apparent that the supplier is having difficulty responding, request a supplier visit to assess compliance.

Unsupported Software or Equipment

There may be equipment and software in use which is no longer supported by a supplier or by the original manufacturer. The method for dealing with these cases will probably depend on the amount of information available, and how difficult it will be to replace the item. If it is a software package and there is a definite Year 2000 problem, it may be possible to fix it. If the source code is not available, the options are reduced. Where the item in question is a piece of equipment with an embedded system, it may or may not be possible determine whether it is Year 2000 compliant. If it is not possible to determine compliance, the criticality assessment will dictate whether or not it will require to be replaced.

Assessing Supplier Responses

Where a supplier has asserted compliance, it is essential to verify this. Asking whether the supplier can demonstrate compliance and, where appropriate, viewing that demonstration, can differentiate between those suppliers which think that they are compliant, and those which know that they are. However, it may be difficult to set up a test environment that will allow a full test of how an application will work over the century change and beyond.

For those PES that are not compliant, it is important to quickly determine when a compliant version will be available, how much it will cost, and what other changes may have to take place in order to achieve compliance.

However, what happens if the supplier does not reply to enquiries, and how much trust can be placed in the reply? The answer in both cases will depend on the criticality of the PES. The more critical the PES, the more effort should be spent talking to the supplier and testing in-house. Some in-house testing will be essential, as it is extremely unlikely that the supplier will have been testing the PES using exactly the same configuration of software or hardware as that which exists on site.

Similarly, where the PES is not compliant and the supplier plans to produce a compliant version by a date in the future that is close to the event horizon of the application, it may be better to find alternatives and plan contingency early on (given that many projects fail to meet time deadlines!).

5.8 FOLLOW-UP REVIEW

Based on the response received from suppliers, there may be potential problems with certain systems and it may be necessary to re-visit the documentation first examined in the Initial Review.

5.9 TESTING DECISIONS

Having established the PES and their criticality assessment, some of the PES being examined should be subjected to triage (deciding the order in which PES are to be subject to Investigative Testing), putting the systems through a mock millennium change and analysing their resultant behaviour.

Bearing in mind the fixed timescales, do not mis-apply expertise, it is too valuable. To this end, decisions should be made on which PES should be subjected to the mock millennium change. This decision-making should be based on triage and should be applied to all PES where a potential failure has been detected:

a) if the PES is going to fail totally (i.e., major problems throughout) do not waste effort on it. Initiate the repair or replacement programme;

b) if you are certain you can survive the nature of the failure and the PES is low criticality, document your acceptance of the problem (or workaround if necessary) and schedule the repair/replacement for a later time once priority items are dealt with;

c) focus on those PES which need immediate attention because:

- they have a high safety criticality score;
- they have a high likelihood of failure;
- significant effort/expertise/time is necessary to effect a repair;
- they have a high business priority.

In planning for Investigative Testing, it may be necessary to accept that:

- this could be a significant project management effort - not only is there a remedial project to manage but this should fit in with other plant/organisational priorities;
- appropriate expertise may be in short supply - but you should use the best people available (despite the costs or impact on other projects);
- the support system may be old, inadequate or missing entirely due to the age of the PES;
- the documentation may be out-of-date, inadequate or non-existent.

5.10 INVESTIGATIVE TESTING

Using the information gained in the audit so far, it is necessary to create a test and inspection schedule which concentrates on the PES identified during Testing Decisions as requiring a mock millennium test. It is important to note that the supplier response should not be the only information used to determine compliance, especially for PES which have a high criticality.

Testing of PES needs to be considered with care, since it carries with it a likelihood of failure. Remember that **if you test it - it may fail**. In producing the test and inspection schedule, assess the impact of failure during Investigative Testing on:

- safety;

- the process;

- the environment (i.e., other dependent systems or processes).

Proceed only when all of the repercussions have been considered, steps have been taken to limit failure effects and there is a contingency plan (if the system proves to be irrecoverable). A HAZOP may be necessary for large processes controlled by safety-related PES. Investigative Testing of a safety-related PES should not be undertaken if the possible consequences of its failure could result in a hazardous event.

Other areas to consider are:-

a) Assess the consequences of testing;

   Off-line is preferable, but be prepared for consequential effects when you re-introduce the PES into service.

   On-line testing should be carried out with great care, and with an acceptance by all of the potential consequences of failure.

b) Ensure that the Backup/Recovery process is in order (it is not unknown for automatic tidy-up routines to delete 'old' data after moving the date forward and wipe out the entire historical storage);

c) Ensure that *at worst* the PES can be re-initialised to a different state (e.g., all storage blanked, all formats at default levels);

d) Use a standby or spare PES if possible;

e) Document the test process and the results (it may be necessary to repeat, or to step back through the process to determine when a fault actually occurred);

f) Supplier demonstrations of compliance may be very useful, especially if they use a representative PES off-line rather than a high-criticality operational PES online.

Testing is not a simple case of setting the date and time to 31 December 1999 and waiting to see what happens when the year changes. There are a number of dates which can potentially cause failure (see Appendix A). Similarly, there are a number of functions of PES which are most likely to cause failure. These include:

a) rollover;

b) trigger dates (generally at the whim of the programmers e.g., 1/1/1, 9/9/99, 1/1/99);

c) date ranges. Software that survives rollover often cannot provide data over a range that spans the year change or even the leap year day;

d) utilities. Tidy up and history handling software can be problematic, especially in database systems;

e) statistics. These may contain date arithmetic;

f) rates. These often use date arithmetic;

g) histories, data archives. These are frequently vectored, i.e., time and date of data change are recorded;

h) audit trails. These date stamp alarms and events and can cause problems when they fail.

5.11 ANALYSIS

The analysis builds on the information produced from the audit, particularly from Testing Decisions and Investigative Testing. From this information, document for each PES contained in the inventory:

- the results of Impact Assessment;

- the results of Testing Decisions;

- the results of Investigative Testing.

For each PES which is known to fail and requires to be corrected, consider all technical solutions. For example, some PES may have more than one option including fix, replace and workaround. The analysis phase should not decide on which corrective action option should be taken - this is part of the strategy and planning stage.

Each technical solution should be documented together with:

- the impact on safety of the technical solution;

- the timescales for the technical solution;

- the cost of implementing the technical solution (and production costs);

- the ease (or difficulty) of the technical solution;

- the acceptance criteria for the technical solution (noting that a partial fix may be acceptable for some PES).

It may also be necessary to define project-specific methods and procedures. For example, these may define the date transfer mechanism between systems.

This stage is completed by producing a report which provides information on all of the above.

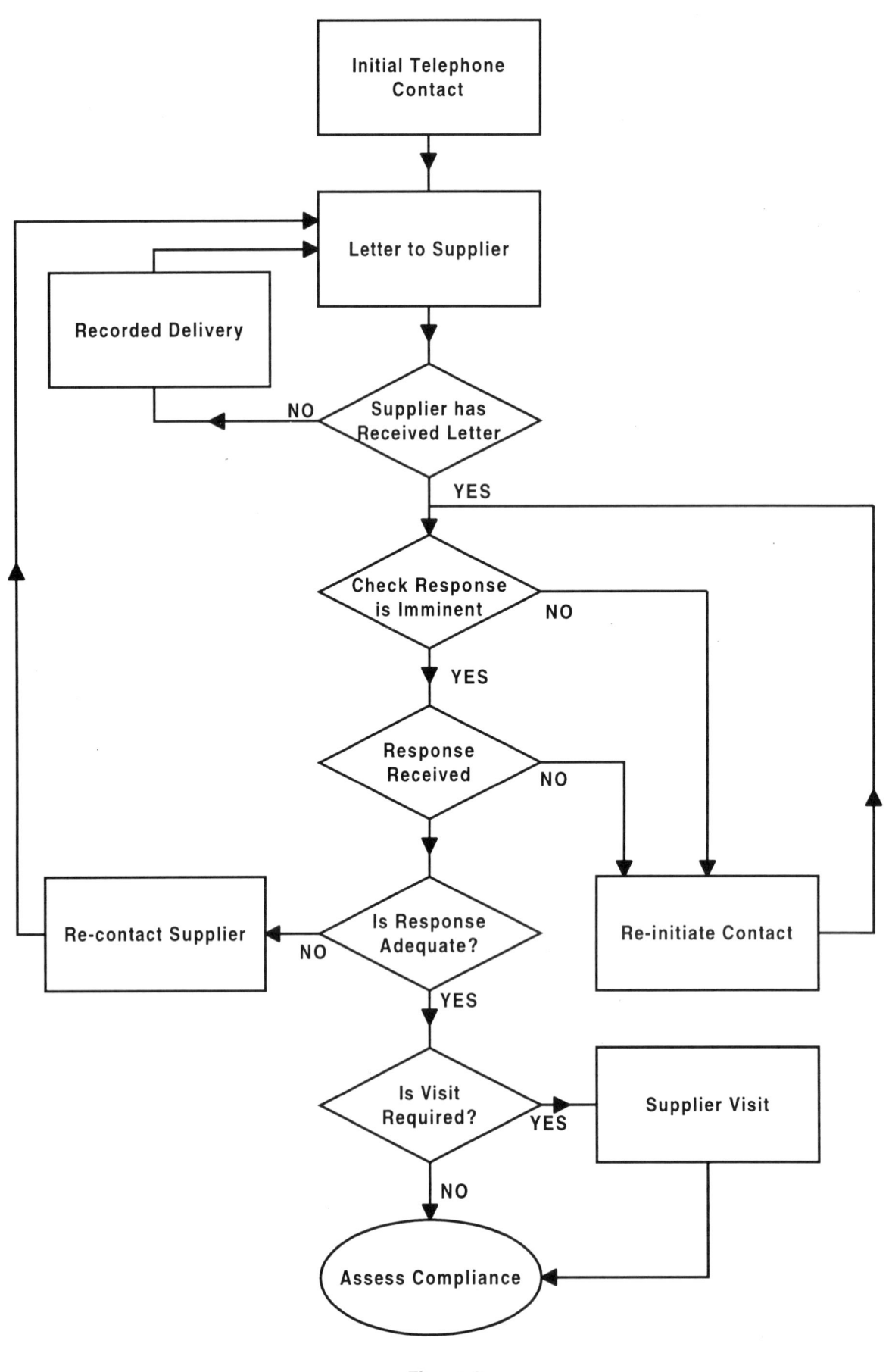

**Figure 6
Supplier Contact**

6. STRATEGY AND PLANNING STAGE

6.1 INTRODUCTION

This section provides guidance on the Strategy and Planning Stage and addresses the following topics:-

- the decision making on how best to tackle the Year 2000 problems and the close co-operation required between staff with different perspectives and knowledge;

- the creation of a comprehensive strategy for the way ahead;

- the creation of a detailed project plan identifying the effects on production, equipment and manpower for each stage of the correction programme;

- acceptance criteria for the various parts of the correction programme;

- methods and working practices for the correction programme;

- contingency planning.

6.2 DECISION MAKING

The time available to deal with a Year 2000 problem (safety or otherwise) is becoming all too short. There is insufficient time for making decisions by consensus among many individuals.

It is recognised that dealing with safety-related issues may be part of an overall Year 2000 programme, and that any remedial actions required will be seen as part of an ongoing plan. However, it is essential that safety-related issues and actions be given sufficient priority to ensure they are dealt with and approved (internally or externally as required) well before the immovable 'crunch' date.

To this end, the overall strategy should be implemented and managed by an individual with sufficient authority to ensure that all necessary tasks are completed. Where necessary, the individual should have the authority to defer other projects with less stringent time pressures. This is generally easier to achieve in small organisations than large ones, but is necessary nonetheless.

Only by a concerted 'team' effort will the necessary plans be put in place and implemented. Dealing with the problem should be seen as a shared responsibility across any company, from the shop floor to the chief executive. It is necessary, therefore, that plans be highly visible and that progress towards the solution be made known to all involved parties.

Within the team, different individuals will have their own perspective on the problems and their part in the overall strategy, but no-one should be in doubt about what is expected of them and the priority of any tasks assigned to them.

6.3 STRATEGIES

The main strategies that may be adopted to minimise or circumvent the Year 2000 problem need to be identified. These include:-

- replace;

- ignore;

- fix;

- work-around;
- revert to manual.

The criticality of the PES should drive the decision on which strategy to adopt for a system. Section 7 contains details of Acceptance Criteria for each of the criticality scores and this may be of use in deciding on the appropriate strategy.

The additional considerations that need to be addressed before choosing the relevant strategy are detailed in the following paragraphs. In adopting any of these strategies, it will be necessary to reassess compliance by generating acceptance criteria and, in many cases, re-testing the PES not only to ensure that the failure is no longer present, but also to ensure that no additional failures have been introduced (not necessarily date related).

6.3.1 Replace

This is on the face of it, the simplest solution. If a PES or PE will suffer from a potential failure - replace it. However, in reality a number of other factors will come into play, e.g.,

- Have all issues relating to safety been adequately covered in terms of:
  - safety functions directly carried out by the PES;
  - the safety integrity of those safety functions;
  - safety PES required to act on the output(s) of the PES (e.g., shut-down mechanisms);
  - instructions related to safe operation of the PES;
  - safe operating ranges (e.g., voltage, pressure, etc.)?
- Is the replacement functionality identical to the original? If not, what is its impact on interacting systems and the overall operation of the process?

6.3.2 Ignore

It may be practical to ignore some potential failures on the basis that safe operation is not compromised. However, consideration should be given to the following:-

- Is the expected failure adequately documented so as not to cause unexpected reactions on the part of the operators of the PES?;
- Will any safety PES react inappropriately because of the failure?;
- Have the results of the failure been fully justified to any necessary authorities (e.g., wrong date on a quality control or maintenance certificate)?

6.3.3 Fix

If a 'Fix' does not result in a complete return to the previous safety performance, functionality and characteristics of the original PES, it should be regarded as a replacement and treated accordingly.

Consideration should be given to whether a fix has been carried out using different support tools than those used in producing the original PES. If so, any resulting new dependencies should be identified, and dealt with as changes to the PES.

Any change to software code, configuration data or logic code should be regarded as an upgrade and require re-acceptance.

6.3.4 Work-Around

A work-around can be purely procedural (e.g., manually mark-up the date on all outputs, or restart the PES every morning) or may involve additional processing of inputs and outputs to the PES. In the latter case, this should be treated as a replacement PES.

If additional operations are required to achieve the work-around, their impact on safety should be assessed.

6.3.5 Revert to Manual

Any reversion to manual operation is subject to a number of considerations:-

- does prolonged manual operation impact on safety in any way?;
- are additional safety procedures or equipment required?;
- when was manual operation last utilised?;
- are there sufficient numbers of competent staff?;
- period of manual operation (and logistics);
- what level of automation has been added since last manual operation?;
- is a task analysis required?;
- is a workload assessment required?

6.4 PROJECT PLANS

Planning a Year 2000 project is difficult. Not only is it a software project (software projects are difficult to plan at the best of times) but there are other factors to consider:

a) Dependency on other systems. It may be that some PES require to be upgraded before others;

b) Production downtime. In some cases, it will not be possible to install and test without shutting the process/plant down. In some plants, this will mean overnight working. In others, it will mean installation and testing during a plant shutdown. During project planning, it may be necessary to schedule additional shutdowns, other than those already planned for preventative maintenance. When installation and testing can be conducted without a shutdown, it will be necessary to ensure that safety cannot be compromised by the testing;

c) Opportunistic Testing. Whilst all test activities will be scheduled in the project plan, there may be occasions when testing can be brought forward. This will probably be as a result of an unplanned shutdown. When this happens, it may be possible to install and test PES which are ready for this stage.

d) Access to Equipment. In common with many projects, a Year 2000 project will require access to live equipment, test equipment, calibration equipment, etc. This should be considered when producing the schedule.

e) Manpower Requirements. A broad range of personnel (from System Specialists to End Users) will be required, and the project plan should take manpower availability into account.

6.5 ACCEPTANCE CRITERIA

It will be necessary to consider the acceptance criteria for each PES and for the operation of the plant as a whole. Section 7 provides more detail on acceptance criteria.

6.6 METHODS AND WORKING PRACTICES

The preferred method for date handling within PES and in interfacing systems should be agreed and documented.

Similarly, a number of new working practices (or changes to existing working practices) may be required. These may be concerned with topics such as:

- maintaining safe operation of plant during installation and test;
- testing of interfaces;
- requirements on suppliers.

6.7 CONTINGENCY PLANNING

The best-laid plans can go astray. Projects associated with computers and software are notoriously difficult to bring in on time, and a Year 2000 programme will be no exception. The programme timescale is additionally risky because it is exceptionally difficult to assess the manpower required, and because industry staff shortages may make it very difficult to secure the numbers of technically-skilled staff needed to ensure a timely project.

For these reasons, contingency plans need to be drawn up in parallel with the main programme plans, or as quickly as possible thereafter. These plans should consider methods by which the organisation can guarantee safety if the rectification programme fails (for whatever reason).

For instance, in these circumstances, it may be possible to maintain safety standards by deploying more staff, perhaps to log information or to perform actions which have previously been computer-controlled. If this is the case, then at what point do these staff need to be employed in order that they can be fully trained and experienced before January 2000?

Alternatively, if a PES is known to be at risk, and the planned fix is running late, perhaps a temporary solution may be to introduce an additional protection PES whose only task is to prevent the PES at risk from taking unsafe actions. At what point in the schedule does the decision need to be taken to specify and purchase the additional protection PES?

Contingency plans should, of course, be continuously re-visited and updated as the programme proceeds in order to guard against the worst-case scenario of being unable to guarantee safe operation in the Year 2000.

7. IMPLEMENTATION AND TEST STAGE

7.1 INTRODUCTION

This stage of a Year 2000 programme is aimed at implementing the prioritised remedial actions which have been identified during the previous stages. As these guidelines are aimed primarily at the safety-related aspects of PES, the highest priority PES to be dealt with will inevitably be those which directly impact on the safety of all concerned. This, in turn, indicates that great care should be taken during these implementation and test activities, which will in all probability have a major impact on production continuity and revenue generation, especially in those organisations concerned with continuous processes.

It has been estimated that up to 60% of the effort involved in a Year 2000 programme will be taken up in testing the remedial actions. Although few organisations have completed this stage as yet, there is little doubt that the effort in testing will be a significant proportion of that allocated to dealing with the Year 2000 problem.

7.2 IMPLEMENTATION PROGRAMME MANAGEMENT

The business of fixing and re-testing PES will often run counter to production efficiency. Amending PES almost invariably means down-time, and the pressure will be on staff to minimise that down-time. This has inherent risks where safety-related PES are concerned. It would be wasteful and dangerous to insufficiently test a revised safety-related PES because of production pressures.

For this reason, it is essential that this stage has hands-on management from a very senior member of the company staff, who has the authority to make decisions when the inevitable conflicts arise between the re-testing programme and the company's production requirements.

At as early a stage as possible, when the extent of the remedial action becomes known, the implementation and test programme should be integrated with ongoing development, scheduled maintenance and production programmes. This should identify where additional effort may be required to maintain safe production and identify any major changes to anticipated business targets as a result.

Testing is a notoriously difficult area to estimate in any project plan, as allowances have to be made for dealing with PES which fail, and require additional implementation and re-test effort. Because of this, immediate decisions may be required which will affect production schedules and other development programmes, in order to achieve the time targets set for priority PES.

7.3 IMPLEMENTATION

7.3.1 Compliance Definition

It is important at the outset to have a clear definition of compliance as related to safety. Normally this would be expected to be based on the BSI definition contained in PD2000-1, amplified to indicate its impact on safe operation, i.e.:

Rule 1- No value for current date will cause any interruption in operation;

Amplification - Interrupted operation should be classified by the impact on safety - the acceptable mechanisms for input and display of the current date should be agreed for each PES;

Rule 2 - Date-based functionality must behave consistently for dates prior to, during and after Year 2000;

Amplification - Consistency in date behaviour has to be defined across all PES, both to ensure that the system behaves safely on all occasions, and that an operator will not be led to an unsafe act by inconsistent date reporting. No safety-related PES should use a date to signify any special function (e.g., 99 = end of file);

Rule 3 - In all interfaces and data storage, the century in any date must be specified either explicitly or by unambiguous algorithms or inferencing rules;

Amplification - In order to ensure safe interpretation, the representation of the date must be defined for each system - preferably a limited set of allowable definitions should be applied to all systems;

Rule 4 - Year 2000 must be recognised as a leap year;

Amplification - No system involved in safety-related activities should be allowed to fail this rule as it is an indication of a flaw in at least its calendar handling.

7.3.2 Rationalising Date Handling

The methods of representation of dates should be reduced to an absolute minimum to ensure that systems or operators cannot be either misled or left in doubt by an ambiguous representation. Either a PES should be implemented based on a full 4 digit year representation or, where a 2 digit date is used, a single, clear definition should be applied (preferably across the organisation) as to the rules for inferring the actual date (e.g. <30 is after 2000, ≥30 is before 2000).

If a PES which reports an incorrect date has to be accepted for whatever reason, the mechanisms used to determine the real date should be reviewed to ensure that no person or PES will react in an unsafe manner to the planned date representation.

7.3.3 Managing Suppliers

If it is necessary to implement a fix from an external supplier, a number of factors should be considered:

- Is the supplier aware of the acceptance criteria that will be applied to the product?;

- Can the supplier demonstrate that the target acceptance criteria have been met before on-site installation?;

- If the fix requires a different operating environment, has this been adequately tested in advance?;

- Have all changes (if any) introduced by the fix been addressed throughout the process to determine the impact on overall safe operation?

Remember that many suppliers will recommend that only the most recent version of their PES can achieve compliance and that this may require other PES to be changed, or may introduce new or changed functionality to the process.

7.3.4 Co-ordinating the Programme

In many cases, an implementation programme will require to be matched to production cycles. This is especially the case when it is required to implement and test PES which can affect safety. Obviously it will be better to schedule such implementation and test at a time which will minimise risk to human safety.

Scheduling such testing during planned shutdowns when a great deal of other activity is going on is not necessarily a safe way to implement changes, although it may be more advantageous in terms of production down-time. Careful consideration should be given as to the safest time to implement changes to safety-related PES (e.g., replacing or upgrading the fire alarm/protection system should not be scheduled during a shutdown when a significant amount of hot-work is scheduled).

It may be necessary to schedule work on safety-related PES when a period of low manning is anticipated. This may mean working overnight where processes are non-continuous or modifying shift rotas to cater for implementation and test.

Obviously the more often that work can be carried out to implement and test a PES in a non-operating environment, the better. However, at some point, it will be necessary to introduce a revised PES into a full operational plant and test it accordingly.

7.4 ACCEPTANCE CRITERIA

In order to achieve the necessary level of compliance on safety-related PES it is necessary to identify the acceptance criteria which should be achieved at each level of safety criticality.

Table 7 gives guidance on how to structure these levels and criteria.

Table 7
Acceptance Criteria

Level of Criticality	Acceptance Criteria	Explanation
High (6)	• Must demonstrate compliance with BSI conformity definition; • Must use the agreed date representation; • Must not fail in a way that will cause unsafe operation; • Must perform all safety-related activities in line with requirements.	Failure of these PES has been assessed as having a high safety risk and therefore no compromise is possible in assessing their correct operation beyond Year 2000.
Upper Medium (4-5)	• Must use agreed date representation; • Must not fail in a way that will cause unsafe operation; • Must perform all safety-related activities in line with requirements.	Although the PES may not comply entirely with the BSI conformity definition, sufficient evidence exists (from testing or supplier demonstration) to determine that all non-conformities have been checked and that either these do not affect safety or other steps have been taken to ensure safe operation.
Lower Medium (2-3)	• Need not use agreed date representation; • Any mis-direction caused by failure has been catered for; • Performs all safety-related activities in line with requirements.	These PES are known to have faults and still have a bearing on safe operation. However, steps have been taken to ensure that safety cannot be compromised.
Low (0-1)	• Does not fail in a way that will cause unsafe operation.	Although the PES may have failures, it has been determined and demonstrated that these cannot lead to unsafe operation. This may be because other mechanisms (manual or automatic) have been put in place to prevent unsafe operation.

These acceptance criteria are suitable when the safety criticality rating is known. It may well be that date related failures in the lower categories may still have a significant impact on business continuity or production efficiency.

7.5 TESTING

A number of steps are required in order to determine whether a PES is acceptable for use once changes have been made to deal with anticipated Year 2000 problems. These steps can be summarised as:-

- Pre-testing Preparation;

- Test Plans;

- Component Level Testing;

- System Level Testing;

- Procedural Validation.

7.5.1 Pre-Testing Preparation

Before beginning any test phase it is essential to ensure that initial planning and preparation for testing is carried out. This is especially true where the PES being tested can impact on safety either by direct action or through failure.

PES judged to have a high criticality rating especially should have a pre-planned testing schedule, which takes into account potential safety hazards which could occur if failure or incorrect action by the PES or operator takes place.

Ideally, all PES with a high criticality rating should be tested off-line in a test-bed environment before being introduced for testing in a 'live' environment. It may be possible to limit such off-line testing to failed components only where the mechanisms by which the components interact with the rest of the PES are well understood. However, complete integration testing of all component parts of a PES will have to be carried out at some point in the programme.

Where a PES performs a direct, safety-related function it is necessary to ensure that alternative methods of ensuring safety are in place during all testing. Alternatively, ensure that the plant on which the PES acts cannot be placed at risk by the act of testing or a system failure due to testing (i.e., it is shut down or safeguarded in some other way).

Where PES failure or test procedures can cause unsafe conditions, all necessary measures to ensure that personnel and plant are not put at risk should be taken. A "Permit to Test" procedure, where all measures are checklisted and agreed before testing, is essential.

7.5.2 Test Plans

Each PES to be tested requires a detailed test plan. This should identify:

- Facilities required to support the test;
- Acceptance criteria to be met;
- Detail of tests to be carried out;
- Safety precautions required during testing;
- Plant state and availability during the tests;
- Expected duration of tests;
- Data to be logged during testing.

All tests carried out successfully should be approved at each stage of the tests, and all steps taken during testing should be logged for subsequent review and audit.

7.5.3 PE testing

Where remedial action has been identified at PE level, then for each PE modified or replaced it will be necessary to:

- Test that PE level failures have been rectified or circumvented;
- Test that the PE functions as per its design requirements;
- Test all PE inter-dependencies within the PES.

7.5.4 PES Level Testing

After completion of PE testing, it will be necessary to integrate replaced components into their respective PES. Test activities should then be carried out to ensure that all failures have been removed, and that the desired safety functionality of the PES has not been impaired. These steps will include:-

- Testing that the safety performance of the system has not been compromised (e.g., safety functions, safety integrity);

- Testing that the PES meets the defined acceptance criteria for Year 2000 operation at its level of criticality;

- Testing that the PES meets its original functional goals (regression testing). This may require re-running original testing carried out during installation;

- Testing that the PES non-functional characteristics (e.g., response times, availability, operation display styles) are within acceptable limits.

7.5.5 Procedural Validation

Before introducing a modified PES into operational service, it will be necessary to:-

- Validate any revised operating or set-up procedures for acceptability;

- Check that any required work-arounds are in place and fully identified to operating and maintenance personnel;

- Ensure that any necessary re-training/instruction of operators and maintainers has taken place.

7.6 YEAR 2000 READINESS

At the time of writing, the majority of firms have yet to complete the Audit and Analysis Stage of a Year 2000 programme for real-time and embedded systems. It is likely that not all identified failures can be remedied in time for the Year 2000.

It is therefore appropriate to consider what is required to achieve 'readiness' for the Year 2000, rather than absolute compliance with all conformity criteria for PES with safety-related aspects.

In order to achieve 'readiness' for the Year 2000 change, an organisation should have:-

- Identified all PES with embedded processors or controlled and/or monitored by processor-based systems;

- Assessed the criticality of the PES in terms of safety;

- Prioritised investigative and remedial action in order to ensure that the failure potential of highest criticality PES has been identified;

- Put a remedial programme in place, which will ensure that all safety-related PES will meet their acceptance criteria in time to test and demonstrate their ability to perform;

- Identified all other PES failures or potential failures in time to take avoidance or contingency steps in order not to overly stress safety PES with undue failure loads;

- Documented all failures that have not been dealt with because it is felt that their failure can be tolerated (this will prevent staff being distracted from safe operation of the plant by unexpected divergence from the norm);

- Ensured that sufficient expertise is available to deal with unidentified Year 2000 failures which may occur.

To achieve "Readiness", an organisation should have reduced the risk of Year 2000 failures to a point where it is certain that safety will be maintained by the application of a variety of the above techniques.

8. RESOURCING THE YEAR 2000 PROGRAMME

8.1 INTRODUCTION

Dealing with the Year 2000 problem is likely to be a drain on the resources of any organisation. Manpower will be expended in planning and managing the programme, undertaking the inventory/audit and analysis work, dealing with suppliers, fixing PES and re-testing them. Safety staff will spend more time than normal in a concentrated period assessing the safety impact of the various options which the rectification programme proposes.

In addition to the manpower impact, there are probable costs associated with purchasing test equipment, or setting up test environments. There may be costs associated with bringing in external technical specialists to assist in the programme. Lastly, there is the prospect that production income will be reduced over the period through essential shutdowns to allow rectification and re-testing work to go ahead.

This section looks at these likely impacts on the resources of the organisations.

8.2 MANPOWER RESOURCES

The internal manpower effort which requires to be expended will vary considerably from one organisation to another. However, in any organisation, there should be commitment to appoint a senior decision-maker to oversee the Year 2000 programme. This individual should be a member of the board of directors, or the board of directors should provide the individual with all of the authorities required to discharge the programme, including the ability to make technical, safety, production and financial commitments on behalf of the organisation.

Most Year 2000 programmes will require the active involvement of safety, systems, production and financial staff, and an early commitment should be made by the directors to free the time necessary for such staff to allow them to make the contribution required to support the programme.

8.3 TEST EQUIPMENT AND TEST ENVIRONMENT

Some costs may be incurred in purchasing (or bringing back into service) the test tools required to undertake Year 2000 testing, and in some cases, the creation of test environments in which existing PES can be subjected to tests without endangering production or safety.

8.4 EXTERNAL TECHNICAL ASSISTANCE

Organisations may decide to bring in external technical assistance if there is insufficient internal manpower resource to undertake the Year 2000 programme. There are obvious cost implications associated with doing so, and these have to be assessed in the light of the risks to safety and, possibly, to business continuity.

However, if the decision is made to bring in external help, it should be noted that there is an existing and predicted shortage of skilled staff available to assist.

In the software services sector, recent statistics suggest that there are 35,000 unfilled IT job vacancies in the UK. The sector has recently been assessed as employing 600,000 staff, and so there is already a 5% shortfall. All industry projections at present suggest that this shortfall will be exacerbated during the run-up to the Year 2000, as more companies recognise the gravity of their Year 2000 problems, and implement rectification programmes.

This shortfall is most likely to have two major effects:-

- it will become increasingly difficult to secure external assistance because of industry shortages;

- the cost of securing external assistance will inevitably increase as the Year 2000 approaches.

Access to external assistance is likely to be more problematic for small and medium-sized enterprises. Larger organisations will be in the position of being able to offer longer contracts, or higher rates, to those who are able to assist. SMEs will find themselves outbid, particularly in geographic areas where the shortages are more acute.

It should also be remembered that PES which contribute to safety (e.g., control systems, protection systems, access/security systems, etc.) represent only a very small proportion of the output of the software services sector, certainly less than 10% of the total. So far from having a pool of 600,000 people to assist, the available number of suitably qualified and knowledgeable staff is a few tens of thousands. Many of these individuals will already be committed to product and service development on behalf of their existing employers and customers, and will not be available to address Year 2000 problems for safety-related PES. The pool of talent is very small indeed, and organisations should not delay if they plan to secure external assistance.

APPENDIX A

DATE DISCONTINUITY

A.1 Introduction

Although the crossover point between 31st December 1999 and 1st January 2000 commands the majority of media attention, creating the terms "Year 2000 Problem" or "Year 2000 Time-Bomb", the time problem revolves around the inability of some systems to handle a variety of dates, not just the midnight hour at the Year 2000.

The inability of a system to handle a date successfully leads to "date discontinuity", and this appendix provides a list of dates which are currently thought to be problematic for some systems.

A.2 Leap Years

Some systems are known not to handle leap years successfully, usually because the algorithm which determines the date has not been correctly programmed. For completeness, and for the avoidance of doubt, the definition by which leap years are determined is as follows:-

- A year is a leap year if it is divisible by 4 (e.g., 1972, 1996)

    unless

- the year is divisible by 100 (1800, 1900 ....) in which case it is not a leap year,

    unless

- the year is divisible by 400 (1600, 2000, 2400 ....), in which case it is a leap year.

A.3 Dates which Require to be Tested

When testing systems for Year 2000 compliance, the following dates should also be tested:-

- 01 January 1999: there are some systems with potential problems because they use 99 as a trigger or as an end-of-file marker. This may be the case if the system handles the year portion of the date as 2 digits;

- 22 August 1999: this is relevant to systems which interface with the Global Positioning System (GPS). The original GPS design allocated a 10-bit register to handle the number of weeks which had elapsed since the base date (or GPS epoch date) of 6th January 1980. The 10-bit week counter will rollover from its maximum value to zero on 22nd August 1999;

- 09 September 1999 (9/9/99): there are some systems with potential problems because they use 9s as an end-of-file marker, i.e., it is the last record in a file or list. New records with "9999" may be construed subsequently as end-of-file;

- 01 January 2000: if a system handles the year portion of the date as 2 digits, actions and calculations may be incorrect;

- 29 February 2000: this is a leap day, and may not appear in some system calendars;

- 01 March 2000: this is the day after leap day. The system may carry erroneous data because of an unexpected leap day;

- 31 December 2000: this is the 366th day, and this has been known to cause problems in systems previously;

- 01 January 2001: this is the day after the 366th day, and the system may carry erroneous data as a result.

When testing these dates, the tests should deliberately encompass the crossover points, i.e., entry to the day and exit from the day at midnight. The tests should not simply ascertain whether or not the system keeps running - many will continue to run, but will produce erroneous results. So comprehensive testing of functionality and data consistency is required at each point.

A.4   Special-to-Purpose Date Testing

When testing for date discontinuity, it is important to consider the functionality of the system. For example, in a recent audit of ship systems, it was discovered that if the operator entered 1/1/1 as the date (i.e., 1st January 2001), the system incorrectly interpreted the entry as a valid command, and switched off access to an important system feature as a result.

APPENDIX B

COMMON AUDIT PROBLEMS

B.1   Introduction

From experience of Year 2000 audits, there are a number of problems which feature in several audits. Typically these problems include the following:

- the existing inventory is not thorough and has either missing PES or sparse information (rendering it ineffective for supplier contact).

- the PES is not accessible for safety/availability reasons. This especially applies to shutdown systems, fire systems, emergency radar systems (GMDSS), 24 hour processes (nuclear, chemical, generator).

- access to documentation can cause serious delays.

- PES can be hidden in the strangest places:

    - either physically in boxes.

    - or virtually, e.g., it was bought under a functional title like "Vibration Analyser" and not controlled or maintained by the IS department (sites that have bought systems through various budgets often "forget" to put them on the inventory).

- Interactions between systems are seldom well-defined.

- Interactions between processes are often forgotten.

- Communications equipment is often overlooked - bridges, routers, terminal servers and managed hubs all contain microprocessors and some are significant computing engines in their own right.

- PLCs often have "BASIC" modules which are effectively Single Board Computers (SBCs) with inbuilt date management capability.

- Suppliers often minimise or fail to understand the problem.

- Suppliers frequently do not reply (some from legal advice).

- Suppliers/manufacturers are no longer trading or have been taken over or have changed names.

APPENDIX C

CASE STUDIES

C.1   Introduction

This section describes some known date discontinuity problems in a variety of systems. Although customers and suppliers have not been named, all of these case studies represent actual Year 2000 problems uncovered during audit and analysis.

C.2   Ancillary Systems

All embedded systems within a facility or plant, whether considered ancillary or not, should be subjected to Year 2000 audit and analysis. Supplier responses should be examined carefully to ensure that they demonstrate an understanding of the totality of potential Year 2000 related failures. The functional role of the system and the systems it can affect should also be fully investigated.

CASE STUDY

A condition monitoring system was initially considered as an ancillary system and declared compliant by the supplier.

On closer examination it was recognised that the condition monitoring system, although ancillary to the production process, performed a regulatory function and that its failure would necessitate the shutdown of the production facilities. This resulted in a significant increase in the assessed criticality of the system.

The system was made up of two processor based components, a data logger and a PC.

Following discussion between Customer and Supplier and in-house testing, several problems were identified:

a) The data logger would not handle the changeover from 31st December 1999 to 1st January 2000. This resulted in the wrong date being assigned to logged data, the consequential generation of a number of incorrectly time stamped events, the failure of the data logger to communicate with the PC and the resultant failure to record time stamped data.

b) The PC date reverted to an earlier date in 1980 resulting in the main trend graph on the PC generating a representation of the period from 1980 to January 2000.

c) Even if the PC had correctly handled the transition from 31st December 1999 to 1st January 2000, there would still have been problems with the graph drawing function caused by the erroneous time-stamping of the data.

This system was referred back to the supplier for further evaluation. A solution to the problem was then proposed by the supplier.

VERDICT

- Examine the supplier's solution very carefully.

- The care and attention necessary in processing all supplier communication is emphasised by this example.

- The Audit and Analysis of supplier responses requires a sound comprehension of both the functional role and the construction of the system under review.

- The rules for determining whether a system is critical or not need to be considered and applied carefully.

C.3 Distributed Control Systems

Distributed Control Systems form an integral part of many facilities.

They also generally contain a significant element of specially written or modified software components in addition to the suppliers' standard facilities found in the baseline product.

Consequently, it might be expected that widely recognised industrial suppliers would be more than willing to co-operate fully with major customers at least.

Unfortunately, this has not been found to be the case for all suppliers. One recognised supplier has already intimated that it currently has no intention of investigating the Year 2000 compliance of its product, nor does it intend to fix any reported problems relating to the product. However, an alternative product is offered for sale which is claimed to be fully compliant.

VERDICT

- An organisation should not rely on all recognised suppliers supplying it with assistance and advice, paid or otherwise, even if it is considered essential for the pursuance of the Year 2000 programme of work. The organisation should determine the willingness and capability of each supplier to provide the required support well in advance of the Year 2000.

- As a result of the assessment of a supplier's readiness and willingness to supply a solution, some systems may have to be developed internally or procured/modified via another supplier. This may well consume time and resources already stretched by other priorities.

- Provision of a significantly revised or alternative version could result in changes to the operation and response characteristics of the package.

C.4 Standard Packages

Commercial Off The Shelf (COTS) packages are widely used throughout the process control and industrial market sectors.

The degree to which a COTS package indicates true standardisation of a product is very much impacted on by its customer base. A package which is sold to less than 100 customers is much more liable to individual tailoring of versions than one which is sold to 100,000 customers. The package with fewer customers is therefore much more prone to variation between implementations.

The costs of Year 2000 related modifications to COTS packages with a small customer base are much more likely to be spread over a small number of upgrades, and are consequently liable to be more expensive.

Some COTS packages also require considerable customisation to meet a customer's requirements. This is likely to result in modifications to the customised parts of the package being one-off costs to be borne by the customer.

Additionally, complications arise where several releases of the standard package are in use across the customer base.

CASE STUDY

The example below highlights complications found with an existing standard package.

An energy monitoring package used by a food producer interfaces to a number of fridge and freezer units. The configuration of the package to support the customer's requirements is primarily screen-based and requires no special software to be written in support of customer sites.

The package is resident on a PC in the engineering office, remote from the units being supervised, and is known by the supplier to be Year 2000 non-compliant. Basic changes need to be made to the package to achieve compliance.

The supplier is offering to upgrade the package at a significant cost to each customer. In addition, the upgraded package is only available on the most recent version of the operating system, thereby forcing a further modification to existing facilities. The upgraded package also contains changed and additional functionality which require a different degree of customisation.

VERDICT

As a customer, you have the following choices.

- Pay up and have the immediate problem resolved.

- Form/join a user group and try to pressurise the supplier to supply at a more advantageous price.

- If time and resources permit, find a new source of supply.

- Be prepared to assess the inevitable changes in operation and functionality which could occur.

C.5 'Hidden' Functionality

Assessment of a system needs an awareness not only of the functional requirement of the system, but also an understanding of the maintenance and support tools embedded within the system.

The identification of such additional or 'hidden' functionality may only arise by inspection of the supplier's documentation or discussion with the supplier's technical or maintenance personnel.

CASE STUDY

A vertical lift system was assessed as failing (though not in a critical manner) as its clock did not roll over correctly from 31st December 1999 to 1st January 2000. On closer inspection, it was found that each movement operation was time stamped and recorded for subsequent up-loading to a hand-held maintenance device.

The clock rollover problem resulted in corruption of the event buffer and a 'buffer full' message was generated. Further lift operations were prohibited by the system until the buffer contents were up-loaded to the maintenance device.

This 'hidden' functionality raised the criticality of this system significantly, as there was no other viable method of lifting essential resources within the facility.

VERDICT

- Never assume that because an element of a system's functionality is unused, it will not cause a problem.

- Criticality assessment should consider the entire operational role, not just the immediate functionality.

C.6 February 2000 and all is well

Having successfully negotiated the transition from December 1999 to January 2000, and having remained operational throughout January, then most people would assume that the problems are over and the Year 2000 programme is complete. Or is it?

As far as possible, all of the potential date discontinuity problems should be analysed and resolved as part of a Year 2000 programme. 29th February 2000 may not be recognised correctly by a number of systems.

29th February 1996 highlighted that systems do not always recognise the occurrence of a 'normal' leap year.

CASE STUDY

Several systems, including a medical scanner, refused to allow entry of this apparently invalid date and refused to allow operation throughout this invalid day.

Several suppliers have already intimated that their systems will not enable users to enter 29th February 2000 as a valid date and that there is no current plan to fix this problem.

VERDICT

- The non-availability of equipment for a day needs as much consideration as other Year 2000 problems.

- If the system concerned does not recognise the entry of 29th February, what date does it produce on the day after 28th February, what day of the week does it recognise thereafter for 'valid' dates, and how many days does it assume to be in the year?

C.7 Global Positioning System (GPS)

GPS is not simply a positioning detection system, but frequently acts as a primary source of position and date/time data for a number of other connected systems.

CASE STUDY

The original GPS design allocated a 10-bit register to handle the number of weeks that had elapsed since the base date (or GPS epoch date) of 6th January 1980. The 10-bit week counter will rollover from its maximum value on the 22nd August 1999. Older models of GPS equipment will revert to some previous date in time, probably 6th January 1980.

Problems occur because the internally held satellite orbital data maintained in the GPS navigator for the erroneous date no longer matches the actual Navstar satellite positions for the new GPS time. The handling of this mismatch will vary depending on the age and design of the receiving GPS unit.

Current position and waypoints processing using the supplied GPS data may be subject to error. Similarly, calculations using this data, e.g., Estimated Time to Arrival will be suspect. The consequence of incorrect positional and routing information needs to be considered carefully.

VERDICT

- Date discontinuity problems are not restricted to Year 2000 issues alone.

- A system that fails at other date thresholds should be considered vulnerable to Year 2000 problems.

- A GPS uses an almanac to correlate positional and date/time information. Almanac calculations are inherently date/time lookups and any inability to handle the Year 2000 dates will cause problems in this area.

C.8 Lifts

Despite uninformed publicity, most lifts will continue to operate safely after the Year 2000, because they contain no date functionality.

CASE STUDY

However, one problem concerning the maintenance chip on certain lifts is known.

When the lift is maintained, the maintenance engineer keys in a keycode to record the maintenance date. After the Year 2000, the date calculations within the maintenance chip, which determine when the lift was last serviced, function incorrectly and the lift ceases operation. The lift is known to fail safe but cannot be used until the maintenance engineer effects a repair (which requires the replacement of the maintenance chip).

VERDICT

- Don't believe all of the scaremongers, but accept that they probably are expanding on a grain of truth.

- Beware of maintenance/diagnostic monitors.

C.9 Exit/Entry Systems

Exit/Entry systems are not limited to those controlling access to a site. In many sites, they control access to restricted, hazardous areas.

CASE STUDY

Some systems have problems because:

- they depend on the day of week to control access. Failure to correctly evaluate the day of week could mean that access to an area is denied;

- some systems, on restart, recover the last known locations of personnel from a file/database. Incorrect interpretation of the last known state (due to recovering the wrong file/database or time stamped records) may mean that personnel are locked in or out of an area. This may have a safety implication;

- the failure of a system may have a standard 'fail-safe' feature which releases all locks. On a hazardous restricted area this is may not be considered to be fail safe.

VERDICT

- Day of the week interpretation inevitably infers date dependency and the potential for failure.

- Fail-safe in some environments may mean the opposite in others.

C.10 Aluminium Smelter Plant

Date discontinuity problems are not restricted to Year 2000 problems. Previous case studies do, however, give us a pointer to the potential for failure contained in date dependence.

CASE STUDY

One of the first documented failures that has already arisen relates to the New Zealand Aluminium Smelters plant at Tiwai Point; all of the smelting potline process control computers stopped working instantly, simultaneously and without warning.

The reason for failure was traced to a faulty computer software program, which failed to take account of 1996 being a leap year. The computer was not programmed to handle the 366th day of the year. Consequently each of the 660 process control computers hung up simultaneously at midnight. Shortly after, as Tasmanian time reached midnight, a sister plant failed in exactly the same way.

The resulting damage to equipment resulted in costs in excess of NZ$1 million.

VERDICT

- Date failures in computer systems are not a new phenomenon.

- Even trivial failures may result in unsafe operation.

C.11 Programmable Logic Controllers

It is inaccurately assumed that simple logic devices such as PLCs will be immune to date related failures. In fact, over 50% of PLCs reviewed in existing studies do contain real-time clocks and date registers.

CASE STUDY

A PLC considered too simple to be worth assessing was found to contain a real-time clock. On investigation it was found intermittently to roll over by 2 years on 31/12/99.

This had little effect on the logic software but caused chaos in the date stamping of events that were essential to failure sequence analysis.

VERDICT

- Even simple controllers can contain non-compliant clock hardware.

- A PLC is only as immune to Year 2000 problems as its application code.

APPENDIX D

SAMPLE LETTERS

D.1   Example 1

Dear <Contact Name (see Figure 6)>,

Year 2000

As you are aware, the advent of the Year 2000 has generated many issues and problems relating to IT systems and automation in industry. In XXXX we are progressing well with a project to investigate the impact and consequences for our own company. We are also keen to promote awareness and stimulate good practice amongst our business partners in terms of recognition of the potential problems and development of precautionary or remedial plans.

One aspect of this project is to determine the status of Year 2000 compliance of the products and services provided by our contractors and suppliers. The basis for compliance is the uninterrupted provision of products and services when dates in and after 2000 are used, including the recognition of 2000 as a leap year. We suggest that our contractors and suppliers consider not only the specific products and services provided, but also consider where reliance on third parties could cause a risk that Year 2000 problems might threaten continuity of operations.

We would ask you to confirm that your consistent delivery of products and services to us will continue into Year 2000 and beyond. If you are unable to confirm this at present, please let us know what plans you have to address the problem.

In our future contracts and purchase orders, we will include a requirement that products and services, which incorporate software, are "Year 2000 compliant". Nevertheless, it is our continued intention to work with our business partners to help to identify the potential problems arising from existing commitments, and to minimise their impact.

We have already made presentations to some of our contractors to outline the problems and the methodology being used by XXXX to identify and prioritise the risks we face. We would be happy to provide similar support to other contractors and suppliers who may be interested.

If you have any further queries on this subject or would like us to explain the issues in more detail please do not hesitate to contact us. All replies should be sent to XXXX.

Yours faithfully

D.2 Example 2

Dear <Contact Name (see Figure 6)>,

YEAR 2000 PRODUCT COMPLIANCE

As you are aware, the Year 2000 issue affects us all.

As part of XXXX Year 2000 Programme, we are reviewing software products, hardware products and general products (which may contain soft or "hard-wired" program code) which are currently in use at XXXX. This work is being carried out on behalf of XXXX.

XXXX uses the product (set) supplied by you which is listed in Appendix A to this letter. We ask you to provide us with details of the compliance of the product (set) and details of the tests carried out on the product (set). These details are of great importance in planning and implementing the Year 2000 Programme.

Please be assured that all information provided will be treated in the strictest confidence and will be used solely for the purpose of ensuring a smooth and successful transition into the next millennium.

It is necessary for the mutual benefit of XXXX and their supplier organisations to act quickly, and it would therefore greatly assist progress of the impact assessment if your reply could be returned to me by <dd-mmm-yyyy>. If you would like to discuss this letter, please do not hesitate to contact me personally on the above telephone number. Otherwise, we look forward to receiving your compliance information.

If you require further information from XXXX, please contact <name> of the <department>.

Thank you in advance for your co-operation in this matter and I hope that we can work towards a successful transition into the 21st century.

Yours sincerely